Developing Teachers' Assessment Literacy

Transgressions: Cultural Studies and Education

Series Editor

Shirley R. Steinberg (*University of Calgary, Canada*)

Founding Editor

Joe L. Kincheloe (1950–2008) (*The Paulo and Nita Freire International Project for Critical Pedagogy*)

Editorial Board

Rochelle Brock (*University of North Carolina, Greensboro, USA*)
Annette Coburn (*University of the West of Scotland, UK*)
Kenneth Fasching-Varner (*Louisiana State University, USA*)
Luis Huerta-Charles (*New Mexico State University, USA*)
Christine Quail (*McMaster University, Canada*)
Jackie Seidel (*University of Calgary, Canada*)
Cathryn Teasley (*University of A Coruña, Spain*)
Sandra Vega (*IPEC Instituto de Pedagogía Crítica, Mexico*)
Mark Vicars (*Victoria University, Queensland, Australia*)

This book series is dedicated to the radical love and actions of Paulo Freire, Jesus "Pato" Gomez, and Joe L. Kincheloe.

VOLUME 134

The titles published in this series are listed at *brill.com/tcse*

Developing Teachers' Assessment Literacy

A Tapestry of Ideas and Inquiries

By

Kim Koh, Cecille DePass and Sean Steel

BRILL
SENSE

LEIDEN | BOSTON

All chapters in this book have undergone peer review.

The Library of Congress Cataloging-in-Publication Data is available online at http://catalog.loc.gov

Typeface for the Latin, Greek, and Cyrillic scripts: "Brill". See and download: brill.com/brill-typeface.

ISSN 2214-9732
ISBN 978-90-04-38565-8 (paperback)
ISBN 978-90-04-38566-5 (hardback)
ISBN 978-90-04-38567-2 (e-book)

Copyright 2019 by Koninklijke Brill NV, Leiden, The Netherlands.
Koninklijke Brill NV incorporates the imprints Brill, Brill Hes & De Graaf, Brill Nijhoff, Brill Rodopi, Brill Sense, Hotei Publishing, mentis Verlag, Verlag Ferdinand Schöningh and Wilhelm Fink Verlag.
All rights reserved. No part of this publication may be reproduced, translated, stored in a retrieval system, or transmitted in any form or by any means, electronic, mechanical, photocopying, recording or otherwise, without prior written permission from the publisher.
Authorization to photocopy items for internal or personal use is granted by Koninklijke Brill NV provided that the appropriate fees are paid directly to The Copyright Clearance Center, 222 Rosewood Drive, Suite 910, Danvers, MA 01923, USA. Fees are subject to change.

This book is printed on acid-free paper and produced in a sustainable manner.

Contents

Notes on Authors VII

Prologue: Developing Teachers' Assessment Literacy: Multiple Perspectives in Action 1
    Kim Koh and Cecille DePass
Structure of the Book 3

1 **Introduction** 7
    Kim Koh
Assessment Literacy: A Universal Construct or a Culturally-Specific Practice? 15
Teacher Preparation and Professional Learning in Assessment 22

2 **Crossing Borders: Navigating Assessments and Evaluations in International Contexts** 27
    Cecille DePass
Part 1: Illustrations of Multiple Perspectives 29
Part 2: Portraits of Education and Assessments 31
Part 3: Re-Examining Cherished Notions of Assessment and Evaluation: A Memory 44
Part 4: Transferability of Academic Credentials: Assessments of Prospective Immigrant Professionals before and after Entering Canada 46
Alberta Network for Immigrant Women Action Research Projects 48
Conclusion 50

3 **A Tale of Two Education Systems** 59
    Kim Koh
Comparative National Contexts 61
Student Performance in International Assessments 64
Redesigning Curriculum for 21st-Century Competencies 66
Assessment, Teaching, and Learning 68
Investment in Teacher Preparation and Professional Development 70
Developing Teachers' Assessment Literacy 75
Recommendations for Teacher Preparation and Professional Development 87

4 **Designing Teacher Education to Promote the Love of Wisdom within a Competency-Based Assessment System**   97
   Sean Steel
   Introduction: The Trend toward Marginalizing Philosophy   97
   The Competencies Movement and Its Impact on Teacher Education   99
   The Third Way: Making Philosophy of Education Core to Pedagogy   102
   Integrating Teaching as a Way of Life   104
   Artful Organization of Philosophy of Education in Competency-Based B.Ed. Learning   105
   Conclusion   111

5 **Looking Forward**   114
   Cecille DePass and Kim Koh
   Fostering Exemplary Assessment Practices: A Problem Scenario   114
   Responses to Dream 1   118
   Responses to Dream 2   119
   Conclusion   120

Index   125

Notes on Authors

Cecille DePass
is a former Commonwealth scholar and Associate Professor Emerita at the Werklund School of Education, University of Calgary in Canada. She taught graduate and undergraduate courses in the University's teacher education programs. DePass has published a number of book chapters and articles in critical pedagogy and multiculturalism. A recipient of the Comparative and International Education Society of Canada (CIESC), David Wilson Award for distinguished services, and The Farquharson Institute of Public Affairs (FIPA), Jamaica, Centennial Award, DePass is a former Chair/President, Education Sectoral Commission, CC-UNESCO. She is the co-editor of *Cultural and Pedagogical Inquiry* which she co-founded.

Kim Koh
is Associate Professor at the Werklund School of Education, University of Calgary in Canada. Prior to joining the University of Calgary, she was Assistant Professor at the National Institute of Education, Nanyang Technological University in Singapore. Kim teaches undergraduate and graduate courses in educational assessment as well as supervises graduate students in educational research. She is the recipient of numerous awards including the University of Calgary Teaching Award for Curriculum Development. Her research is focused on teachers' assessment literacy and teachers' capacity in the design and use of authentic assessment. Her work has been supported by several major grants such as the University of Calgary Teaching and Learning Grant, the Alberta Education Research Partnership Grant, and the Social Sciences and Humanities Research Council (SSHRC) Insight Grant. Kim has published numerous peer-reviewed journal articles, book chapters, and books (*Improving Teachers' Assessment Literacy, Mastering the Art of Authentic Assessment, Vols. I & II, Authentic Assessment in Schools*). She has served as Program Chair of Division D Measurement and Research Methodologies of the American Educational Research Association.

Sean Steel
is a public school teacher as well as a former sessional instructor and lecturer at the Werklund School of Education, University of Calgary, Ambrose University, and the Southern Alberta Institute of Technology (SAIT) in Canada. Sean has published broadly in the fields of education, philosophy, religion, politics, and law. His books include *The Pursuit of Wisdom and Happiness in Education*

(SUNY Press, 2014), *Teacher Education and the Pursuit of Wisdom* (Peter Lang, 2018), *Suffering and the Intelligence of Love in the Teaching Life: In Light and in Darkness* (Palgrave-Macmillan, 2019), and most recently *Plato's Myth of Er: A Personal Journey Re-Told by ELL and Refugee Students* (Eaglespeaker Publishing, 2019).

PROLOGUE

Developing Teachers' Assessment Literacy: Multiple Perspectives in Action

Kim Koh and Cecille DePass

Assessment for learning (AfL) has been touted as a key lever for improving instructional practice and student learning in light of global education reforms that place greater emphasis on the provision of equitable learning opportunities for all students to learn and master essential competencies such as critical thinking, complex problem-solving, effective collaboration, communication, and self-directed learning. These competencies (i.e., 21st-century competencies) are of paramount importance in the global knowledge-based economy, which requires considerable numbers of educated workers who can perform sophisticated, non-routine skills (Darling-Hammond & Adamson, 2010). As such, many education systems around the world have invested in reforming K–12 school curricula to incorporate content and performance standards that reflect the importance of students' learning and demonstration of a blend of these competencies. Teachers in K–12 schools are deemed to play a pivotal role in realigning their instructional and assessment practices to the competency-based curricula.

Since the beginning of the 21st century, K–12 teachers have been urged to adopt alternative forms of assessment (e.g., authentic assessment, performance assessment, formative assessment, assessment for learning) that align with the reformed vision of curriculum (Shepard, 2000). However, teachers' successful adoption and implementation of alternative forms of assessment depends on their levels of assessment literacy. Put simply, assessment literacy refers to a teacher's understanding of sound classroom assessment practices (Stiggins, 1991). A substantial body of literature has emphasized the importance of developing preservice and inservice teachers' assessment literacy. In fact, teachers' demonstration of assessment literacy or competence is one of the key professional standards for teacher certification, licensure, and evaluation in many education systems around the world. Hence, initial teacher preparation programs are expected to provide high-quality assessment curricula to preservice teachers so that they are well equipped with essential assessment knowledge and skills prior to their entry into teaching. Likewise, inservice teachers who lack assessment preparation during their preservice teacher education programs need to be supported by the provision of high-quality professional development programs that build their assessment capacity.

As the act of teaching has become increasingly demanding and complex, we hope that developing teachers' assessment literacy is more responsive to the needs of preservice and inservice teachers from linguistically and culturally diverse backgrounds. We concur that both preservice and inservice teachers in today's educational contexts require a deeper understanding of assessment, such as knowing the purposes and functions of different kinds of assessment. Additionally, teachers are urged to appreciate the history of educational assessment and know how to determine the merits of a range of assessment practices best suited for their lesson planning and classroom teaching.

Active involvement in the design, selection, and use of authentic assessments (i.e., performance assessments or performance-based tasks that are authentic or rich tasks) is the best strategy to support teachers in realigning their instructional and assessment practices. As Wyatt-Smith and Gunn (2009) stated, "It was the assessment that challenged the teacher to rethink the pedagogy—'a massive pedagogical leap'—expected to flow on to improved outcomes" (p. 91). This suggests that improving teachers' assessment literacy will enable teachers to adopt innovative pedagogical and assessment methods that help promote the development of higher-order competencies (or essential competencies or 21st-century competencies) in K–12 students. Students' mastery of competencies is essential because it will prepare them to meet their future college and workplace demands (Darling-Hammond & Adamson, 2010). However, extant research has clearly shown that teachers in many education systems around the world lack assessment literacy due to their inadequate preparation in classroom assessment at the preservice level (e.g., DeLuca & Klinger, 2010; Koh, 2011; Mertler, 2009; Popham, 2008, 2009, 2011; Stiggins, 2002; Volante & Fazio, 2007). Hence, developing teachers' assessment literacy has become a key initiative in initial teacher preparation and inservice teacher professional development programs which aim to promote excellence in teaching with an ultimate goal of improving student learning.

The term "assessment literacy" was first coined by Stiggins (1991) to describe teachers' understanding of the basic principles of sound assessment practice. These principles include having clear assessment purposes, assessing performance of multiple skills, establishing a good fit between assessment tasks/methods and curricular goals, and using reliable, fair, and valid assessment approaches. According to Willis, Adie, and Klenowski (2013), "Assessment literacy will be understood differently depending on the view of learning embedded in the cultural and policy context and so is closely associated with theories of learning" (pp. 244–245). As Luke (2011) aptly noted in his 2011 AERA

(American Educational Research Association) distinguished lecture, "Policy borrowing can only begin from a consideration of local cultural context, historical genealogy, and contending ideologies" (p. 375). Similarly, teachers' assessment literacy needs to be articulated and explicated based on both their views of learning and their conceptions of assessment, which are shaped by local cultural, social, and political influences. One size does not fit all. As such, it is important for teacher educators, researchers, policymakers, and other education stakeholders to consider the differences in historical, sociocultural, and geopolitical contexts of each education system while formulating and implementing policies and strategies for developing teachers' assessment literacy.

Structure of the Book

In this book, we discuss significant aspects of developing teachers' assessment literacy in initial teacher preparation and inservice teacher professional development programs. Kim Koh, the lead author, has considerable research and teaching experience in three post-colonial countries: Canada, Singapore, and Malaysia. Over ten years of her career, she has been actively involved in designing assessment courses for both preservice and inservice teachers and teaching both groups of teachers in two of the aforementioned countries. Her co-authors, Cecille DePass and Sean Steel, based on their different educational backgrounds and teaching and scholarly experiences, bring multiple perspectives to the contested field of assessment and evaluation. Cecille DePass brings the perspective of more than 20 years of post-secondary teaching and an inquiring eye regarding education in the Caribbean and Canada. Sean Steel offers a philosopher's view, enriched from his instructional experience in Canadian schools and initial teacher preparation programs. At one point, their paths crossed fortuitously; all three taught at the same time in the same preservice teacher education program at a western Canadian university.

Based on their respective academic and applied fields of work, Koh invited each co-author to produce a chapter for the emerging book. Yet, typical of academic replies to such requests, the chapters submitted for inclusion in the book prove to be widely different. Each is a critical response to the topic of assessment, which presents the complexity of the subject through a breadth and range of content and perspectives. By expanding the terms of reference regarding assessment, the authors have developed a book with a far richer panorama on assessment as a springboard for inquiry.

Each author tackles the central issues in markedly different ways. However, the commonalities underpinning their respective contributions diverge and converge in intricate patterns. This is similar to that of the mighty rivers which flow eastwards from the Rocky Mountains and have helped to carve the changing, post glacial plains of the western prairie geography of Alberta, Canada. Notions of learning assessment and evaluation have changed, too. Each author conveys a perspective of assessment, learning, and teaching that has changed over time as circumstances, knowledge, and understanding have changed. The authors present multiple historical, sociocultural, and geopolitical perspectives, from China to ancient Greece to the former British Empire and contemporary Singapore and Canada. Each author explains personal encounters with assessment and evaluation to examine "what happens in assessment." As well, Kim Koh, Cecille DePass, and Sean Steel map the purposes and functions of assessment and highlight the impact of assessment on learners and teachers. Like the rivers of the Rocky Mountains alluded to above, each chapter carves its own path only to converge and become part of an intricate pattern. With each chapter, the authors unite to challenge the reader by emphasizing alternative ways to consider assessment, its implementation, and its role in education.

For organizational and structural purposes, the book is presented as a series of artistic tapestries. The symbol of tapestries, hopefully, encourages viewing each chapter as a strikingly unique, yet complementary artwork that engenders inquiry into the key issues and themes identified above. In Chapter 1, Kim Koh brings the tapestries to life for readers. She introduces a study replete with the silken threads of traditional Asian embroidery in which she defines and explores assessment literacy in terms of its research, policy, and practice contexts.

Using bold colors in her tapestry patterns, in Chapter 2, Cecille DePass provokes critical thinking to explore assessment and evaluation in international and historical contexts. The chapter examines some key assumptions, implications, and impacts of assessment and evaluation policies and practices on stakeholders. In so doing, the chapter untangles the threads associated with such concepts as universality and transferability of assessment and evaluation. DePass concludes with reference to one of the United Nations' (UN) universal declarations that promote education for all people, including women and girls, in economically developing countries.

Steeped in the classics, Sean Steel presents highly detailed tapestry patterns in which Sophia, the Greek goddess of wisdom resides. In Chapter 3, he critiques the demise of philosophy of education in initial teacher preparation programs and offers suggestions for future thinking, discourse, and practice. Steel patterns explicate seminal questions and perspectives which contest contemporary notions of assessment. The chapter questions underlying suppositions of reliance on preparing preservice teachers for competencies. It explores how such preparation shapes preservice teachers' attitudes toward educating for inquiry and the pursuit of wisdom. Steel encourages a shift in one's thinking and practice.

In Chapter 4, Kim Koh continues to weave, with precision, greater levels of detail. The emerging pattern flowers in ways similar to a cluster of beautiful peonies offering intricate layers of petals. The chapter presents a comparative analysis of developing teachers' assessment literacy in two high-performing education systems: Alberta (Canada) and Singapore. Students in both education systems rank high in international assessments (i.e., Program of International Student Assessment, Trends in International Mathematics and Science Study). The chapter synthesizes recent educational reforms, policies, and practices, as well as teacher preparation and professional development in both education systems that strive to maintain a competitive edge in a global knowledge economy.

Finally, in Chapter 5, we present a problem scenario and its solutions. Our aim is not to provide preordained recommendations. Rather, the problem scenario serves as a way to invite discussion on strategies for developing teachers' assessment literacy given global education reforms and current trends in educational assessment and teacher education.

References

Darling-Hammond, L., & Adamson, F. (2010). *Beyond basic skills: The role of performance assessment in achieving 21st century standards of learning.* Stanford, CA: Stanford University, Stanford Center for Opportunity Policy in Education.

DeLuca, C., & Klinger, D. A. (2010). Assessment literacy development: Identifying gaps in teacher candidates' learning. *Assessment in Education: Principles, Policy & Practice, 17*(4), 419–438.

Koh, K. (2011). Improving teachers' assessment literacy through professional development. *Teaching Education, 22*(3), 255–276.

Luke, A. (2011). Generalizing across borders: Policy and the limits of educational science. *Educational Researcher, 40*(8), 367–377.

Mertler, C. A. (2009). Teachers' assessment knowledge and their perceptions of the impact of classroom assessment professional development. *Improving Schools, 12*(2), 101–113.

Popham, W. J. (2008). *Transformative assessment.* Alexandria, VA: Association for Supervision and Curriculum Development.

Popham, W. J. (2009). Assessment literacy for teachers: Faddish or fundamental? *Theory into Practice, 48*, 4–11.

Popham, W. J. (2011). Assessment literacy overlooked: A teacher educator's confession. *The Teacher Educator, 46*(4), 265–273.

Shepard, L. A. (2000). The role of assessment in a learning culture. *Educational Researcher, 29*(7), 4–14.

Stiggins, R. J. (1991). Assessment literacy. *Phi Delta Kappan, 72*(7), 534–539.

Stiggins, R. J. (2002). Assessment crisis: The absence of assessment for learning. *Phi Delta Kappan, 83*(10), 758–765.

Volante, L., & Fazio, X. (2007). Exploring teacher candidates' assessment literacy: Implications for teacher education reform and professional development. *Canadian Journal of Education, 30*(3), 749–770.

Willis, J., Adie, L., & Klenowski, V. (2013). Conceptualising teachers' assessment literacies in an era of curriculum and assessment reform. *Australian Educational Research, 40*, 241–256.

Wyatt-Smith, C., & Gunn, S. (2009). Towards theorizing assessment as a critical inquiry. In C. Wyatt-Smith & J. J. Cumming (Eds.), *Educational assessment in the 21st century: Connecting theory and practice* (pp. 83–102). Dordrecht: Springer.

CHAPTER 1

Introduction

Kim Koh

Schön (1983, 1987) has long advocated that reflection upon one's own experience can improve one's own practice. His work has led to a worldwide adoption of reflection or reflective practice as a pedagogical approach in both initial teacher preparation and inservice teacher professional development programs. The ability to reflect enables individuals to self-assess the deep-seated assumptions governing their behaviors or actions; identify the historical, social, cultural, and political origins of the assumptions; and challenge these assumptions in order to develop better or alternative ways of doing or practice (Cranton, 1996). According to Brookfield (2017), it is through critical reflections, teachers are able to construct new knowledge and insights that help transform their professional practices. In view of the need to transform my own professional practice as a teacher educator, I begin this chapter with my own reflections on my experiences of assessment and on how they have impacted my conceptions of assessment. More important, how my conceptions of assessment have evolved from when I was a student to when I became a teacher educator and how my conceptions are influenced by the historical, sociocultural, and policy contexts of each of the following nations: Malaysia, Canada, and Singapore. An understanding of my own conceptions of assessment will also enable me to design effective assessment curriculum and pedagogical strategies for developing teachers' assessment literacy in the context where I teach.

As a third-generation Chinese Malaysian, I was born and grew up in a small town in Malaysia. My grandparents were Chinese immigrants who came to Malaysia in the 1930s due to political and economic turmoil in Mainland China. My parents were born in Malaysia, and Teochew, a Chinese dialect, was my first spoken language at home. English was the fourth language I learned as a compulsory subject at both elementary and secondary schools. For most students in Malaysian public schools, the purpose of learning English is to pass the subject in high-stakes national examinations. A post-colonial country, Malaysia is located in Southeast Asia. According to the 2018 Census, over 60% of the 32.4 million Malaysian population are Malays and indigenous people, 20.8% are Chinese, 6.2% are Indians, and 10.4% are non-citizens. Since independence in 1957, the Malay language has been the official language in all government sectors and functions. It is also used as the medium of instruction in all public schools and higher education institutions (Gill, 2005).

My elementary and secondary education both took place in public schools and I completed my bachelor's and master's degrees in a public higher education institution in Malaysia. At the time, there were only seven public universities. At the tertiary and postgraduate levels, almost all the reference books were in English. As such, we students were required to do our readings in English and to write our assignments and examinations using the Malay language. A turning point of my education was being awarded a Canadian Commonwealth Scholarship, which enabled me to pursue my doctoral study in Canada. I will reflect on my Canadian experience later in this chapter.

During elementary school, I admired the work of my teachers; as such, I grew up determined to become one. I remember being fascinated by how my teachers delivered their lessons using colorful textbooks, as well as how they marked students' worksheets, workbooks, tests, and examinations using stars and marks as rewards. After each summative test or end-of-term examination, I was eager to discover how well I had performed by looking at the marks or grades. The response formats in many of my assignments (in-class or homework), tests, and examinations were predominantly multiple-choice or selected-response, matching, true-false, or fill-in-the-blanks. In hindsight, I attributed my stellar academic performance to my strong working memory, which was designed by God. This working memory enabled me to regurgitate facts and procedures despite facing other challenges when I was a child. Additionally, a strong desire to overcome poverty and racial discrimination led me to work diligently and excel in all my tests and examinations. I also learned several test-taking strategies from my teachers (e.g., how to cancel out poorly-written distractors from a multiple-choice test).

At the end of each school term, my form teacher used "blue ink" to register the marks I attained in all subjects, including arts and physical education, on my report card, indicating that I had not failed any of them. My report card also registered the number of days I attended during each school year. I was proud of having only one day of absence from my elementary school education. At the end of each school year, all students were ranked based on their aggregate scores across all the school terms. For my teachers and me, all classroom assessments were summative and only served accountability purposes, such as determining annual class ranking, promotion to the next grade, classroom placement, or awards.

Once I entered secondary school, I had to adjust to a new learning environment and catch up with the official language (i.e., Malay) which was used in all public schools in Malaysia as a medium of instruction in all academic subjects except English. I was exposed to assignments, tests, and examinations that employed more constructed-response items, which required me to construct my own responses rather than select only one correct answer from a range of preordained options. However, I could still rely on my mental capacity to memorize facts and procedures in solving most of the routine problems. Classroom assessment did not appear to support student learning, since all the assignments given to us were designed to help us digest new information so we could perform well in national examinations. Over the course of five years, I sat three high-stakes national examinations[1]; the pressure was enormous because my performance in these examinations determined my future academic major and career pathway. Since the implementation of affirmation action policy in Malaysia in 1971, the ethnic majority Malays have received preferential treatment in business permits and grants, real-estate ownership and civil service employment, admission to universities and teacher training colleges, and scholarship to local and overseas institutions (Guan, 2005). Selection of applicants for university admission in Malaysia was based only on students' aggregate scores derived from five academic subjects (Malay language was a compulsory subject) which they undertook in their Malaysian version of Cambridge A-Level exam. The Malaysian government not only set quotas for the admission of ethnic minority Chinese and Indian students into its public universities, but also implemented race-based differential standards for determining students' subject specializations and career pathways. To secure a place at university, ethnic Chinese and Indian students who sat for the Cambridge A-Level exam were expected to have higher aggregate scores than their Malay counterparts and also achieve a good grade in the Malay language subject. As a result, many of my talented classmates and close friends who were ethnic Chinese did not meet the admission standards, and this curtailed their hopes and opportunities. Their predicament corresponds to what Gipps (1999) writes about the politics of assessment,

> The "owners" of examinations, whether ministries of education, boards of examiners, or private agencies, possess power over important resources and decisions ... Poor examination results may deny students access to certain levels and forms of advanced schooling and thus close the doors to social, political, and economic advancement. (p. 366)

In short, my first 12 years of formal education conditioned and reinforced rote memorization and passive learning. Classroom assessment and student learning were conceptualized based on a behaviorist learning approach (Skinner, 1948) that reinforced desired performance through rewards or sanctions.

All the worksheets, workbooks, and tests were given by my teachers with an eye toward preparing students for success in high-stakes national exams. As a result, students were often driven by a performance mindset rather than a growth mindset. The former is associated with the view that an individual's intelligence or mental capacity is innate or fixed, while the latter "is based on the belief that your basic qualities are things you can cultivate through efforts" (Dweck, 2006, p. 7). Students who hold a performance mindset neither believe in efforts nor perceive that learning is a progression. As such, they give up and lose interest easily while encountering the first few failures. They may also perceive learning and assessment as a threat to their self-esteem and end up having a low level of self-efficacy. In contrast, students who hold a growth mindset will persist and demonstrate the same high level of interests in solving problems and overcoming challenges because they believe in hard work and perceive that learning is a progression.

Most standardized tests and examinations employ item formats that are constrained in nature and hence only allow for measuring students' attainment of lower-order learning outcomes. Heavily relying on academic performance that is predominantly measured by standardized tests reduces opportunities for students to develop their non-academic skills such as critical thinking, creativity and innovation, complex problem-solving, self-directed learning, collaboration, and communication. These are the so-called 21st-century skills and competencies deemed essential in a competitive global marketplace (Partnership for 21st Century Skills, 2002) and vital for individuals who wish to find success in their personal, social, and civic life. They are best captured by authentic and performance assessments, as well as being cultivated through assessment for and as learning practices. These alternative forms of assessment will be the central focus of our discourse in the following chapters of the book.

In hindsight, I must admit that my ability to memorize facts and procedures, as well as my diligent work ethic, helped me excel in all high-stakes national examinations and sail through many storms during my undergraduate studies. As undergraduate students, my course mates and I were asked to complete term papers, projects, and a graduating thesis. Although these tasks were designed as authentic performance assessments, they were used merely as summative assessments for accountability purposes. Little was known about the impact of the performance assessments on both our careers and personal lives.

I began my first academic job as an assistant instructor at one of the Malaysian public universities at the end of the 1990s. When I reflected on my two-year teaching experience at the university, I must admit that I was very comfortable with my adoption of the traditional didactic lecture approach and summative assessment because they enabled me to have better control over my classroom and students' learning. Similar to my teachers and instructors, I expected all my students to follow my instructions and to perform well in exams. Thus, my conception of assessment was aligned with a behaviorist learning approach and a psychometric testing paradigm that placed a greater emphasis on objective measures of student performance (e.g., standardized multiple-choice tests) and norm-referenced grading practice. At the time, many educators did not perceive assessment as an integral part of teaching and learning. Students were seldom given the opportunity to engage in critical inquiry beyond the textbook.

In fall 1998, I began my doctoral studies in Canada, where there was a very different academic culture. To my surprise, I was exposed to a new philosophy of education. In classes, instructors encouraged, if not expected, graduate students to actively engage in asking questions and making arguments. It was the first time I had learned the importance of communicating my ideas, thoughts, and opinions not only in writing but also orally in front of my professors and peers. It was a cultural shock, as the professors who had taught me during my undergraduate study had not expected students to ask questions in class, and neither had I when I began my first faculty position. In fact, silence and compliance were considered virtues that good students must possess and demonstrate during class time. As one of the eastern cultures, the "chalk and talk" pedagogical approach and standardized testing method seemed to fit better with the Malaysian professors' and students' conceptions of assessment and learning at the end of the 20th century.

Although my course mates and I were actively involved in classroom discourse in most of our doctoral courses in Canada, our academic achievement was predominantly measured by how well we performed on weekly assignments, mid- or final-term examinations, and final-term papers. Unlike current assessment practices in higher education institutions, graduate students in the late 1990s and early 2000s in Canada and elsewhere were seldom exposed to the use of rubrics. Therefore, the assessment criteria and standards used for summative assessments were forever mysterious. Our instructors seemed to know best in grading students' assignments, examinations, and papers. Graduate students seldom asked what an A grade actually meant and how we could work toward meeting the expectations of an A paper. Completion of a doctoral dissertation was one of the key indicators of success in graduate school, yet little was known about the assessment criteria and standards. Supervisors held the criteria of quality work in their heads. Graduate students received constant formative feedback and only learned from their supervisors whether their dissertations had met expectations and whether their dissertations were ready for external examination and final defense. Supervisors were also regarded as experts in a field and were highly respected by their graduate students who perceived themselves to be apprentices. Such an apprenticeship model made most graduate students feel humble to learn from their supervisors who also served as lifelong mentors.

As an international graduate student in a highly competitive PhD program, my goal was to excel in academic performance despite the pressure of a language barrier and other life challenges. In retrospect, I think my own measures of academic success were narrowly defined because I equated them to the good grades I obtained and the number of scholarships I received. However, I had greatly benefited from my PhD supervisor's and committee members' dedicated supervision and mentoring which helped transform my thinking about academic success and its assessment. They provided me with research assistant opportunities, where I learned how to conduct high-quality educational research for the public good. They also mentored me in co-authoring and co-presenting scholarly papers at peer-reviewed conferences, and in co-publishing journal articles. Without their dedicated tutelage and mentorship, I would not have had a strong curriculum vitae nor done well in my interview for a faculty position in one of the higher education institutions in Singapore. Taken together, these suggest that the measurement of academic success needs to be multi-dimensional (e.g., good grades, scholarships, publications, knowledge mobilization at conferences, communication) and involve a wide variety of assessment methods.

When I resumed my academic career at the beginning of the 21st century, the terms "authentic assessment," "portfolio assessment," "formative assessment," and "assessment for learning" had begun to dominate the field of education. These alternative forms of assessment are aligned with a social-constructivist paradigm of student learning and are deemed effective for promoting students' learning and mastery of the 21st-century competencies. These competencies include critical thinking, complex problem-solving, collaboration, communication, self-directed learning, grit, and resilience, as well as information and communication technology (ICT) literacy. Many scholars have advocated for these forms of alternative assessments to replace traditional standardized paper-and-pen tests (e.g., Black & Wiliam, 1998a; Newmann, Marks, & Gamoran, 1996; Shepard, 2000; Stiggins, 2002; Wiggins, 1989). Standardized tests are aligned with a behaviorist view of learning and are often used for summative assessments to fulfill accountability demands (e.g., certification, selection, rewards/sanctions). Additionally, the item formats used in standardized tests were predominantly multiple-choice, selected-response, true-false, matching, fill-in-the-blanks, and short answers. Such formats reinforce students' recall of discrete facts and routine procedures. The emphasis is on arriving at the correct answer based on memorizing and reproducing what has been learned from textbooks. Knowledge is decontextualized, and students' meaning-making is less of a priority during the transmission of knowledge from the expert to the novice. In other words, knowledge in a subject or discipline is perceived as a fixed body of "transmitted," memorizable facts and routine procedures rather than an active, collaborative, innovative, and creative construction of new concepts, ideas, and solutions by either the student or the student and his or her peers (Newmann et al., 1996). I still remember how I had to make a lateral shift in my conception of assessment from a psychometric orientation to a sociocultural orientation. The psychometric orientation aligns with a behaviorist epistemology while the sociocultural orientation is in sync with socioconstructivism. When I first joined a research center at one of the Singaporean universities, I was asked by my former Dean Professor Allan Luke, a world-renowned sociologist of education, to lead a research project evaluating the quality of teachers' assessment tasks and the quality of students' work in Singapore grades 5 and 9 classrooms. The new concepts "teacher-moderated assessment" and "rich tasks" were introduced to me. Additionally, a project manager passed me a few artifacts that the research associates/assistants had collected from the classrooms where they had done their coding of teachers' lessons. Our research findings indicated that the quality of students' work was dependent on the quality of assessment tasks set by teachers. The findings corresponded to those from Fred Newmann's Chicago School Reform Study (Newmann, Marks, & Gamoran, 1996) and Bob Lingard and Allan Luke's Queensland School Reform Longitudinal Study (Lingard et al., 2001). Reading Newmann et al.'s authentic intellectual work and Lingard et al.'s productive pedagogy and assessment was an eye-opening experience. It had a positive impact on my thinking about assessment, pedagogy, and student learning, and their relationship. In hindsight, my first "on-the-job" research training and mentorship by Allan Luke, one of the giants of educational sociology in the 21st century, enabled me to reflect on and challenge my own assumptions of assessment. One of the recurring questions I asked myself was: Why I didn't perceive assessment as an integral part of teaching and learning before? My design and development of a graduate course "Mastering the Art of Authentic Assessments," which I also taught for eight years to inservice teachers, school administrators, and nursing instructors at the National Institute of Education Singapore has helped me reaffirm my belief in a sociocultural approach to assessment, teaching, and learning, despite my strong passion in using measurement principles in my research. Since becoming a faculty member in a Canadian context, such belief has greatly influenced my work with both preservice and inservice teachers.

In short, as a student, three-quarters of my education occurred under the influences of the behaviorist learning approach and standardized testing. My first teaching experience as a university instructor was still under the influence of the same philosophy. In contrast, when I re-entered the academic world after my graduate study, my pedagogical and assessment approaches were influenced by the worldwide education reforms at the turn of the 21st century. These reforms advocated a shift toward a social-constructivist learning approach and alternative, authentic assessment. Educators or teachers who believe in social-constructivist learning theory perceive that constructing new knowledge and developing cognitive abilities or intellectual capabilities are primarily facilitated by social interactions within the learning environment. This is in line with Vygotsky's (1978) sociocultural approach to cognitive development. According to Vygotsky, students can develop higher-order thinking skills through working on a challenging task with assistance from the teacher or a competent peer within the zone of proximal development. Such teacher or peer assistance was first coined "scaffolding" by David Wood, Jerome Bruner, and Gail Ross (1976) in their classic text "The role of tutoring in problem solving." Scaffolding needs to be removed gradually when students demonstrate task mastery during the learning process. This will support them in becoming independent learners.

Teachers' beliefs, conceptions, and practices are often influenced by their previous educational experiences (Kagan, 1992; Richardson, 1996) and the cultural, social, and political contexts where they reside (Brown, 2011). Research consistently shows that preservice teachers' past learning experiences influence how they think and act during teaching as well as how they interpret instructional practice (Bullough, Knowles, & Crow, 1992; Connelly & Clandinin, 1988; Pajares, 1992). Additionally, the formation of their beliefs can be influenced by other factors, which include familial and cultural understandings, and interactions with formal knowledge of subject matter (Richardson, 1996). Taken together, I believe it is not easy to change one's preexisting beliefs and notions of teaching, learning, and assessment. Hence, it has taken more than a decade for me to shift my beliefs and conceptions regarding assessment, teaching, and learning, which has transformed my instructional and assessment practice. My assessment literacy has evolved over time and across varied and contrasting educational contexts. The gradual shift of my conceptions of assessment leads me to inquire whether policies and strategies for developing teachers' assessment literacy can be transferred from one sociocultural and political context to the other. To address this question, it is worthwhile to examine the construct of "assessment literacy" as follows.

Assessment Literacy: A Universal Construct or a Culturally-Specific Practice?

The term "assessment literacy" has become a buzzword (but an important one) in initial teacher preparation and inservice teacher professional development programs since it was first coined by Richard Stiggins (1991). According to Stiggins, assessment literacy refers to mastering the basic principles of sound assessment practice. In his seminal article published in *Phi Delta Kappan*, assessment literacy was further defined as knowing "the difference between sound and unsound assessments" (Stiggins, 1995, p. 240). Stiggins (1995) used five standards to characterize teachers' sound assessment practices. The standards include (1) clearly articulating assessment purposes and learning goals; (2) establishing clearly defined achievement targets; (3) properly selecting or designing assessment methods that match identified learning goals and that capture desired achievement targets; (4) representative sampling of student achievement or performance; and (5) avoiding bias and distortion in assessment. Each standard is worth considering in teacher education and professional development to help prepare preservice and inservice teachers for exemplary classroom practices. Stiggins's (1995) definition of assessment literacy applies to both standardized paper-and-pen tests and alternative forms of assessment (e.g., authentic assessments, performance tasks).

Assessment literacy is key to transforming instructional practice and student learning in today's classrooms. Hence, teachers need to develop assessment literacy. To support teachers' development of assessment literacy, Stiggins (2001) called for school leaders (i.e., principals) to be assessment-literate. Stiggins (2002) also pointed out that a lack of assessment for learning practice in K–12 classrooms was a threat to students' development of both academic (i.e., mastery of core subjects) and non-academic skills (i.e., 21st-century competencies). Almost a decade later, Popham (2009) stated that assessment-literate teachers made better instructional decisions and adopted better classroom assessments, which led to improvements in teaching and student learning. In essence, both Stiggins and Popham emphasize teachers' learning how to use classroom assessments to support their instructional practices and students' learning. According to Chappuis and Stiggins (2002), assessment for learning or formative assessment can have positive effects on student learning and achievement because it focuses on using day-to-day classroom assessment to engage and motivate students in the learning process. Assessment for learning can promote students' growth mindsets, that is, awareness that learning is a progression rather than a fixed ability or single event rewarded by success and punished by failure. Additionally, teachers need to use formative classroom assessment data to reflect on their instructional practices and adjust their teaching activities with an eye toward supporting students' learning.

To redefine excellence in assessment, Stiggins (2006) called for striking balanced assessment systems at the classroom, school, district, state, and national levels. To do that, each stakeholder, including students, teachers, parents, school administrators, policymakers, and community members, needs to understand the purposes and functions of different types of assessments. In essence, there is a need to balance assessment for learning, assessment as learning, and assessment of learning practices. As such, it is of paramount importance for teachers to learn and master a repertoire of assessment strategies for use with students in the contemporary classrooms. Stiggins is one of the prominent educational assessment researchers in the US calling for the provision of assessment for learning opportunities for K–12 students.

The Stiggins (1995) standards are well suited for classroom teachers. A few other educational assessment standards are more comprehensive and developed by professional organizations to guide the assessment practice of a broader group of stakeholders, including test developers and users, school administrators, teachers, policymakers, and researchers. For example, the Standards for Educational and Psychological Testing were published by the American Educational Research Association (AERA), the American Psychological Association (APA), and the National Council on Measurement in Education (NCME) in 1999. It is deemed to be a benchmark for guiding measurement and testing practices in the US. The International Test Commission has also promoted the Standards to other countries. In 2014, a revised version of the Standards (AERA, APA, & NCME, 2014) was published to include four additional aspects relating to assessment: accountability issues for the use of tests in educational policy, accessibility of tests for all examinees, a more comprehensive role for tests in the workplace, and an expanded role of technology in testing. Although the revised Standards manual is widely adopted by both researchers and practitioners in the educational measurement community, its applicability to teacher preparation may be limited because of a heavy focus on developing, validating, and using standardized tests. As well, technical aspects (e.g., reliability, validity, comparability) of the Standards focus may make them less appealing to teachers and school administrators.

Prior to the Standards for Educational and Psychological Testing, the American Federation of Teachers, National Council on Measurement in Education, and National Education Association (AFT, NCME, & NEA, 1990) published the 1990 Standards for Teacher Competence in Educational Assessment of Students. The Standards consist of a comprehensive set of assessment knowledge and skills which can be a guideline for developing teacher candidates' competence in educational assessment. They also serve as a benchmark for teacher educators, teachers, professional developers, and researchers (Brookhart, 2011). In 2011, Brookhart updated the 1990 Standards to reflect two major assessment trends. First, the update included a fine-grained conception of formative assessment that includes students' use of formative assessment to support learning (i.e., assessment for learning), and second, teachers' competence in formative assessment or assessment for learning. The revised Standards were also included in educational assessment textbooks (e.g., Nitko & Brookhart, 2011). In 2015, the Joint Committee for Standards on Educational Evaluation released Classroom Assessment Standards: Practices for K–12 Teachers (Klinger et al., 2015) for use with teachers, students, school administrators, and parents/guardians. The ultimate goal of the Standards is to support student learning.

In the United Kingdom, Black and Wiliam (1998b) have long advocated for formative assessment or assessment for learning as a way to empower both teachers and students in using classroom assessment to improve learning. Their systematic meta-analysis of 250 empirical studies revealed a strong and positive effect of formative assessment on student achievement. Since then, Black and Wiliam's (1998b) work has been highly cited by educational researchers around the world. Teachers' competence in formative assessment or assessment for learning was deemed the most important skill in teachers' day-to-day instructional practice. As such, it was added by Susan Brookhart (2011), an influential author in classroom assessment, to her list of assessment knowledge and skills that redefines the term "assessment literacy." Based on her study of more than 200 experts in education and an analysis of major teacher assessment initiatives in the United Kingdom, Harlen (2010) proposed ten principles of high-quality assessment, which correspond to Stiggins's (1995) five standards of quality assessment (see Table 1.1).

Compared to Stiggins (1995), most of Harlen's principles are associated with assessment for and as learning. Stiggins's (1995) standards apply to both assessment for accountability and learning, while Harlen's (2010) principles lean toward the ultimate goal of using all types of assessments to support student learning. Harlen's principles echo Lorrie Shepard's (2000) socio-constructivist view of assessment and learning. In her seminal article, "The Role of Assessment in a Learning Culture," Shepard, former president of the American Educational Research Association, pointed out the importance of realigning classroom assessment to a reformed vision of curriculum. The article was written as the world entered into the 21st century. At the time, there was a clarion call for shifting from traditional standardized testing toward alternative forms

TABLE 1.1   Comparison of Stiggins's Standards (1995) and Harlen's Principles of High-Quality Assessment (2010)

Stiggins (1995)	Harlen (2010)
Clearly articulate assessment purposes and learning goals/learner outcomes	– All assessments should aim for improving student learning (i.e., assessment for and as learning) – Assessment should enable and motivate students to demonstrate what they know and can do through the use of authentic assessments – Assessment should help key stakeholders (e.g., students, parents, the public) have a better understanding of learning goals relevant to students' current and future lives
Establish clearly defined achievement targets	– Assessment should be an integral part of the teaching and learning process in which students are helped to understand their learning goals and the criteria used to judge the quality of their work or performance (i.e., success criteria and performance standards in a rubric) – Assessment methods should promote students' motivation and active engagement in the learning process (e.g., assessment as learning including self-assessment, reflection, metacognitive strategies) – Assessment methods should meet agreed-upon standards for quality assessment practice at all levels (from classroom to systemic level)
Properly select or design assessment methods	– Assessment methods should enable the facilitation and reporting of students' progress pertaining to all essential learning goals. To do so, assessment methods need to match the intended learning goals.
Have a representative sampling of student achievement, work, or performance	– Assessment should include multiple sources of information/data, including students' self- and peer assessment, to inform important decisions about students' learning and achievements
Avoid bias and distortion in assessment	– Assessment procedures should include explicit processes to ensure that information or data gathered from students are reliable and valid – Assessments of learning outcomes are subject to unavoidable measurement errors. Hence, assessment results need to be interpreted with caution.

of assessment in light of global curriculum reforms that place greater emphasis on developing K–12 students' 21st-century competencies or capabilities.

In Canada, another North American education jurisdiction, the Principles for Fair Student Assessment Practices for Education (Joint Advisory Committee, 1993; Rogers, 1996) have served as guidelines for both assessment developers and users to ensure fair and equitable assessment for all students. Based on the Standards for Teacher Competence in Educational Assessment of Students (AFT, NCME, & NEA, 1990), the Principles for Fair Student Assessment Practices for Education in Canada consist of five broad interrelated themes: "developing and choosing assessment methods, collecting assessment information, judging and scoring student performance, summarizing and interpreting results, and reporting assessment findings" (Joint Advisory Committee, 1993, p. 3). Under each of the broad themes, the following clearly defined standards and principles are established:
– alignment of assessment methods to instructional objectives or learning goals;
– validity of inferences about students' knowledge, skills, and dispositions drawn from assessment information;
– assessment methods should be free of bias in terms of language, culture, and students' prior experience;
– judgment of student work or performance should be based on transparent scoring guides/rubrics; procedures for summarizing and interpreting assessment results must yield accurate and informative representations of a student's work or performance; and
– assessment reports need to be clear, accurate, and useful for the intended users.

The Canadian principles and standards for fair student assessment practices align with Stiggin's (1995) standards of quality assessment. Since its inception, the Principles for Fair Student Assessment Practices for Education has been widely adopted by researchers, practitioners, and policymakers all across Canada.

In Australia, using a sociocultural lens, Willis, Adie, and Klenowski (2013) argued for defining teachers' "assessment literacy" as a dynamic social practice that is context-dependent and involves "teachers articulating and negotiating classroom and cultural knowledges with one another and with learners, in the initiation, development and practice of assessment to achieve the learning goals of students" (p. 242). This means teachers' competence to engage in intellectual discourse with colleagues on assessment practices and to promote student-centered assessment in the day-to-day classroom is of utmost importance.

Drawing on Bernstein's (1999) concepts of vertical and horizontal discourse and classification and framing, Willis et al. (2013) distinguished between the nature of discourse concerning conventional and alternative forms of assessment. Conventional assessment is characterized by summative assessment or assessment of learning, which encompasses standardized testing and emphasizes uniform test administration and objectivity in scoring procedures. Hence, conventional assessment is reflective of the characteristics of Bernstein's (1999) vertical discourse, which includes strong framing and classification (i.e., the teacher has more control over classroom discourse and use of metaknowledge, and specialized rules and procedures). This type of discourse is commonly found in classrooms where didactic pedagogical approaches are employed by teachers to transmit knowledge to students. The two most frequently used didactic pedagogical approaches are whole-class lectures and I.R.E./F. (teacher initiation, student response, and teacher evaluation/evaluative feedback). I.R.E./F. was first coined by Courtney Cazden, a world-renowned sociolinguist and Professor Emerita at the Harvard Graduate School of Education, to describe student-teacher talk in K–12 language arts and mathematics classrooms (Cazden, 2001). I.R.E./F. classroom discourse is consistent with summative assessment of learning in which teacher evaluation or feedback is focused on the personal level or directed to the "self" (Hattie & Timperley, 2007, p. 90). This form of feedback is evaluative in nature and is not related to students' performance on the task. Examples include "Well done," "Good job," and "Try harder." They are not informative enough to help improve students' learning and performance.

In contrast, alternative forms of assessment, including authentic assessment, performance assessment, formative assessment or assessment for learning, assessment as learning, stealth assessment, and game-based assessment reflect the characteristics of Bernstein's (1971) horizontal discourse that values teachers' critical inquiries into their own assessment practices and students' learning processes. According to Cazden (2001), there is a need for teachers to place "more emphasis on process and strategies for learning and doing" (p. 5). Teachers are also encouraged to be more reflective in their classroom teaching. This can be done through teachers' reflections on their own teaching practices or teachers' self- or collective analysis of the video clips of their own teaching episodes, for example, Japanese Lesson Study (Lewis, 2002) and video study of mathematics teachers' instructional practice (e.g., Koh, 2015).

Both aspects of assessment discourses are influenced by teachers' views and beliefs about student learning, which are often shaped by teachers' prior educational experiences and the local cultural and political context where teachers reside and practice. According to Willis et al. (2013), teachers who are assessment-literate need to be competent in moving between multiple assessment discourses in the daily classroom teaching and learning context. Hence, they posit that assessment literacy is not a singular or fixed set of capabilities. Rather, it is a capability that is context-dependent and "needs to be understood within the assessment culture and policy context of the community" (p. 246).

Clearly, assessment literacy is defined in many ways. Most definitions center on teachers' knowledge of and skills in designing, selecting, and using assessments for various purposes, such as designing and using authentic assessment or performance assessment to capture higher-order learning ouctomes or competencies. Teachers' assessment knowledge and skills also include analysis, interpretation, and use of assessment data for both summative and formative purposes. Summative assessment refers to using assessment information or data for accountability. For example, assessment data are used to determine student placement at the end of a school year. Summative assessment is synonymous with assessment of learning. Formative assessment, or assessment for learning refers to using assessment information or data to inform teachers' instructional practice and support students' learning throughout the learning process. At the foundation of these definitions, assessment literacy is a universal construct which signifies that teacher preparation and professional development programs should aim to develop an assessment skill set in pre-service and inservice teachers, respectively. This skill set is focused on teachers' declarative knowledge or "know-what" and procedural knowledge or "know-how" technical skills. Hence, such a skill set may be deemed common across different education systems irrespective of sociocultural and policy contexts.

In this book, we question the validity of defining "assessment literacy" as a universal construct across different sociocultural and policy contexts. This aligns with Willis et al. (2013), who contend that teachers' assessment literacy is a dynamic social practice which is context-dependent and involves teachers' active learning of sound assessment practices through intellectual discourse and collaborative work with their peers in a collegial and supportive professional learning community (PLC). For example, when teachers look together at students' work in school-based PLC sessions to analyze and understand students' reasoning and misconceptions, it suggests a dynamic social practice rather than a passive implementation of a fixed set of technical knowledge and skills. Forming such a learning community encourages teachers to learn and master new assessment knowledge and skills, as well as share exemplary assessment practices in a supportive and collegial learning environment (Wiliam & Thompson, 2008). Over the past decade, many professional development programs have shifted away from one-shot, ad hoc workshops. Rather, they were designed and implemented as ongoing, sustained, school-based

PLCs in which teachers actively engaged in conversations about instructional and assessment practices.

Teacher Preparation and Professional Learning in Assessment

Over the past two decades, developing teachers' assessment literacy has been touted as a mechanism for improving the quality of teaching, assessment, and learning in K–12 schools. One of the greatest concerns in various countries is that many inservice teachers have low levels of assessment literacy due to inadequate assessment preparation in their preservice teacher education programs (DeLuca & Klinger, 2010; Koh, 2011; Koh & Luke, 2009; Mertler, 2009; Stiggins, 1995; Volante & Fazio, 2007). In Canada, DeLuca and Klinger (2010), as well as Volante and Fazio (2007), have called for developing preservice teachers' or teacher candidates' assessment literacy in initial teacher preparation programs. This is consistent with Popham (2009), who recognized the fundamental role of teacher education and professional development programs in developing preservice and inservice teachers' assessment literacy in the US. He stated, "Teachers who are genuinely [assessment] literate will not only know how to create more suitable assessments but will also be conversant with a wide array of potential assessment options" (p. 7). In many countries, both preservice and inservice teachers are given ample professional learning opportunities to learn and master a wide range of assessment methods and strategies. In fact, teachers' demonstration of assessment literacy is listed as one of the key competencies in professional standards for teacher certification, licensure, and evaluation in some education systems (e.g., US, Canada, Singapore).

In conclusion, extant research in educational assessment, curriculum, and teacher education has consistently pointed out that professional learning and support are needed for developing teachers' assessment literacy with an ultimate goal of improving student learning. A key aspect of assessment literacy is designing high-quality assessment tasks to intellectually engage K–12 students, with an eye toward promoting their learning and mastery of 21st-century competencies (Koh, Burke, Luke, Gong, & Tan, 2018). These competencies include critical thinking, creativity and innovation, complex problem-solving, collaboration, communication, self-directed learning, grit and resilience, and information, communication, and technology (ICT) literacy. They are the much-needed skill set in contemporary global society that emphasizes knowledge production, digital literacy, and developing a strong science, technology, engineering, and mathematics (STEM) workforce. Many of the aforementioned competencies are hard-to-measure constructs, which means they can only be tapped by observing in real-world contexts and exercising teachers' professional judgment

(Klenowski & Wyatt-Smith, 2010; Stiggins, 1995; Wiggins, 1989). Hence, teachers' capacity to design, select, and use quality authentic assessment tasks (i.e., authentic performance tasks) is essential for creating equitable opportunity for students to demonstrate their competencies or capabilities in day-to-day classroom teaching and learning.

In many high-achieving education systems around the world, deliberate efforts have been invested in the design and development of assessment curriculum and resources for use with preservice and inservice teachers in teacher preparation and professional development programs. Such efforts will ensure that both preservice and inservice teachers are well equipped to teach and assess 21st-century competencies in light of the global education reforms. In Chapter 3 of this book, we intentionally included a cross-cultural comparison of developing teachers' assessment literacy in Alberta (a western province of Canada) and Singapore, which are two of the high-performing education systems in international assessments. The two cases serve as our best attempt to address three fundamental questions. First, can policies and strategies for developing teachers' assessment literacy be transferred from one educational context to the other? Second, can similar assessment curriculum and resources be developed and used for developing preservice and inservice teachers' assessment literacy across different sociocultural and political contexts? Finally, given an enormous interest in supporting teachers and teacher candidates to use assessment to promote teaching and learning, how can we, as teacher educators and educational researchers, move beyond the rhetoric of developing teachers' assessment literacy?

Note

1 In Malaysia, these national examinations included SRP, SPM, and STPM. SRP was a lower-secondary summative assessment at the end of Grade 9. SPM, a high-stakes national exam in Grade 11, was equivalent to the Cambridge O-Level, while STPM was equivalent to the Cambridge A-Level, a pre-university exam, which served as the sole criterion of admission to Malaysian universities and for the university assignment of academic major to students. All the exam papers (except for the English subject) in these high-stakes national exams were written in the Malay language.

References

American Educational Research Association, American Psychological Association, & National Council on Measurement in Education. (2014). *The standards for educational and psychological testing*. Washington, DC: Authors.

American Federation of Teachers, National Council on Measurement in Education, National Education Association. (1990). *Standards for teacher competence in educational assessment of students*. Retrieved from https://files.eric.ed.gov/fulltext/ED323186.pdf

Bernstein, B. (1999). Vertical and horizontal discourse: An essay. *British Journal of Sociology of Education, 20*(2), 157–173.

Black, P., & Wiliam, D. (1998a). Assessment and classroom learning. *Assessment in Education: Principles, Policy & Practice, 5*(1), 7–74.

Black, P., & Wiliam, D. (1998b). Inside the Black box: Raising standards through classroom assessment. *Phi Delta Kappan, 80*, 139–148.

Brookfield, S. (2017). *Becoming a critically reflective teacher* (2nd ed.). San Francisco, CA: Jossey-Bass.

Brookhart, S. M. (2011). Educational assessment knowledge and skills for teachers. *Educational Measurement: Issues and Practice, 30*(1), 3–12.

Brown, G. T. L. (2011). Teachers' conceptions of assessment: Comparing primary and secondary teachers in New Zealand. *Assessment Matters, 3*, 45–70.

Bullough Jr., R. V., Knowles, J. G., & Crow, N. A. (1992). *Emerging as a teacher*. New York, NY: Routledge.

Cazden, C. B. (2001). *Classroom discourse: The language of teaching and learning* (2nd ed.). Portsmouth, NH: Heinemann.

Chappuis, S. C., & Stiggins, R. J. (2002). Classroom assessment for learning. *Educational Leadership, 60*(1), 40–43.

Connelly, F. M., & Clandinin, D. J. (1988). *Teachers as curriculum planners*. Toronto: OISE Press.

Cranton, P. (1996). *Professional development as transformative learning: New perspectives for teachers of adults*. San Francisco, CA: Jossey-Bass.

DeLuca, C., & Klinger, D. A. (2010). Assessment literacy development: Identifying gaps in teacher candidates' learning. *Assessment in Education: Principles, Policy & Practice, 17*(4), 419–438.

Dweck, C. S. (2006). *Mindset*. New York, NY: Ballantine Books.

Garet, M. S., Porter, A. C., Desimone, L., Birman, B. F., & Yoon, K. S. (2001). What makes professional development effective? Results from a national sample of teachers. *American Educational Research Journal, 38*(4), 915–945.

Gill, S. K. (2005). Language policy in Malaysia: Reversing direction. *Language Policy, 4*(3), 241–260.

Gipps, C. (1999). Socio-cultural aspects of assessment. *Review of Research in Education, 24*, 355–392.

Guan, L. H. (2005). Affirmation action in Malaysia. *Southeast Asian Affairs*, 211–228.

Harlen, W. (2010). What is quality teacher assessment. In J. Gardner, W. Harlen, L. Hayward, & G. Stobart (Eds.), *Developing teacher assessment* (pp. 29–52). Maidenhead: Open University Press.

Hattie, J., & Timperley, H. (2007). The power of feedback. *Review of Educational Research, 77*(1), 81–112.

Joint Advisory Committee. (1993). *Principles for fair student assessment practices for education in Canada.* Edmonton: Centre for Research in Applied Measurement and Evaluation, University of Alberta.

Kagan, D. M. (1992). Professional growth among beginning and preservice teachers. *Review of Educational Research, 62*, 129–169.

Klenowski, V., & Wyatt-Smith, C. (2010). Standards, teacher judgement and moderation in contexts of national curriculum and assessment reform. *Assessment Matters, 1*, 84–108.

Klinger, D., McDivitt, P., Howard, B., Rogers, T., Munoz, M., & Wylie, C. (2015). *Classroom assessment standards for prek–12 teachers: Joint committee on standards for educational evaluation.*

Koh, K. (2011). Improving teachers' assessment literacy through professional development. *Teaching Education, 22*(3), 255–276.

Koh, K. (2015). The use of video technology in pre-service teacher education and in-service teacher professional development. In S. F. Ng (Ed.), *Cases of mathematics professional development in East Asian countries* (pp. 229–247). Singapore: Springer.

Koh, K., Burke, L. E. C. A., Luke, A., Gong, W. G., & Tan, C. (2018). Developing the assessment literacy of teachers in Chinese language classrooms: A focus on assessment task design. *Language Teaching Research, 22*(3), 264–288. doi:10.1177/1362168816684366

Koh, K., & Luke, A. (2009). Authentic and conventional assessment in Singapore schools: An empirical study of teacher assignments and student work. *Assessment in Education: Principles, Policy & Practice, 16*(3), 291–318.

Lewis, C. (2002). *Lesson study: A handbook of teacher-led instructional change.* Philadelphia, PA: Research for Better Schools.

Lingard, B., Ladwig, J., Mills, M., Bahr, M., Chant, D., Warry, M., Ailwood, J., Capeness, R., Christie, P., Gore J., Hayes, D., & Luke, A. (2001). *The Queensland school reform longitudinal study.* Brisbane: Education Queensland.

Mertler, C. A. (2009). Teachers' assessment knowledge and their perceptions of the impact of classroom assessment professional development. *Improving schools, 12*(2), 101–113.

Newmann, F. M., Marks, H. M., & Gamoran, A. (1996). Authentic pedagogy and student performance. *American Journal of Education, 104*, 280–312.

Nitko, A. J., & Brookhart, S. M. (2011). *Educational assessment of students* (6th ed.). Boston, MA: Pearson.

Pajares, M. F. (1992). Teachers' beliefs and educational research: Cleaning up a messy construct. *Review of Educational Research, 62*(3), 307–332.

Partnership for 21st Century Skills. (2002). *Learning for the 21st century skills: A report and MLE guide on 21st century skills.* Retrieved from http://www.p21.org/storage/documents/P21_Report.pdf

Popham, W. J. (2009). Assessment literacy for teachers: Faddish or fundamental? *Theory into Practice, 48*, 4–11.

Richardson, V. (1996). The role of attitudes and beliefs in learning to teach. In J. Sikula (Ed.), *Handbook of research on teacher education* (2nd ed., pp. 102–119). New York, NY: Macmillan.

Rogers, W. T. (1996). Principles for fair student assessment practices for education in Canada. *Assessment in Education: Principles, Policy & Practice, 3*(3), 397–400.

Sciön, D. (1983). *The reflective practitioner*. London: Temple Smith.

Sciön, D. (1987). *Educating the reflective practitioner*. San Francisco, CA: Jossey-Bass.

Shepard, L. (2000). The role of assessment in a learning culture. *Educational Researcher, 29*(7), 4–14.

Skinner, B. F. (1948). 'Superstition' in the pigeon. *Journal of Experimental Psychology, 38*(2), 168–172.

Stiggins, R. J. (1991). Assessment literacy. *Phi Delta Kappan, 72*(7), 534–539.

Stiggins, R. J. (1995). Assessment literacy for the 21st century. *Phi Delta Kappan, 77*(3), 238–245.

Stiggins, R. J. (2001). The principal's leadership role in assessment. *NASSP Bulletin, 85*, 13–26.

Stiggins, R. J. (2002). Assessment crisis: The absence of assessment for learning. *Phi Delta Kappan, 83*(10), 758–765.

Stiggins, R. J. (2006). *Balanced assessment systems: Redefining excellence in assessment*. Portland, OR: Educational Testing Service. Retrieved from http://oea.dpi.wi.gov/files/oea/pdf/redefine.pdf

Volante, L., & Fazio, X. (2007). Exploring teacher candidates' assessment literacy: Implications for teacher education reform and professional development. *Canadian Journal of Education, 30*(3), 749–770.

Vygotsky, L. S. (1978). *Mind in society: The development of higher psychological processes*. Cambridge, MA: Harvard University Press.

Wiggins, G. (1989). A true test: Toward more authentic and equitable assessment. *Phi Delta Kappan, 70*, 703–713.

Wiliam, D., & Thompson, M. (2008). Integrating assessment with learning: What will it take to make it work? In C. A. Dwyer (Ed.), *The future of assessment: Shaping teaching and learning* (pp. 53–82). New York, NY: Lawrence Erlbaum Associates.

Willis, J., Adie, L., & Klenowski, V. (2013). Conceptualising teachers' assessment literacies in an era of curriculum and assessment reform. *Australian Educational Research, 40*(2), 241–256.

Wood, D., Bruner, J. S., & Ross, G. (1976). The role of tutoring in problem solving. *Journal of Child Psychology and Psychiatry, 17*(2), 89–100.

CHAPTER 2

Crossing Borders: Navigating Assessments and Evaluations in International Contexts

Cecille DePass

Processes of formal education, assessments, and evaluations are inextricably linked in a series of complicated, interlocking, and overlapping networks which involve a sizable number of stakeholders. The stakeholders range widely, from members of international and national assessment and testing syndicates and organizations to policymakers and administrators in nation-states. For instance, in Canada, federal and provincial governments play significant roles (Ghosh & Ray, 1991) as do university researchers in public and private institutions, foundations and think-tanks, parents, schools' principals/heads, administrators, and teachers. Finally, at the core of education initiatives are the students who should be the subjects, in Paulo Freire's (1987, 1972) terms.

For descriptive and analytical purposes, discussions of formal assessment in different international contexts are central to this writer's contribution to the book. A guiding assumption regarding education systems is recognizing and accepting that in the big picture, a society's fundamental assumptions, core values, beliefs, ideologies, and visions of its future are explicitly and/or implicitly illustrated in the formal grading, testing and examining of its students, who are tomorrow's citizens and leaders.

Assessments are effectively sanctioned forms of social control used to facilitate sociocultural, political, and economic mobility. They are administered and usually accepted by most stakeholders as delineated above. Assessments and evaluations are screening procedures which occur at specific stages as one progresses through the hierarchical ladders associated with public or private schooling. As importantly, assessments and screening procedures are sanctioned and embraced by students who continue to universities and other post-secondary institutions as well as by the few who eventually pursue doctoral or postdoctoral degrees. Further, for many students who accept and excel in the existing forms of assessments and evaluations (i.e., summative assessments or assessment of learning), the educational process grants emancipation from ascribed restrictions of race, ethnicity, class, and gender (Yvonne Brown, personal communication, April 3, 2017).

The "Crossing Borders" contribution to the book presents a series of symbolic portraits of assessments and evaluations in a few countries. To do so, it adopts a full palette of colors, and the author uses several brushes. For example, students' and immigrant professionals' narratives of lived experiences are depicted in vivid colors. Another broad brushstroke advances secondary sources (some classic, some contemporary) that illustrate (when blended with more finely nuanced strokes) key issues, dilemmas and impacts associated with assessments and evaluations that influence students' lives. The contribution explores and represents portraits, pictures, and sketches of some of the major problematics and complexities associated with formal assessments and evaluations within and across different cultural and national contexts. It highlights the sense of agency in terms of selected responses by some stakeholder students and parents.

The chapter consists of five major parts, each of which includes several metaphorical paintings to provoke the reader to take another glance at assessment. Part 1 contains two well-known fables which I have embellished considerably to illustrate multiple perspectives. The first, a classic Asian fable, portrays the many-sidedness of phenomenon. The second, dependent on the narrator, has origins attributed to Latin American, Indian, and European folklore. For the most part, accepting Jagruti Dolakia's (1994) version, I sketch, in considerable detail, some key aspects of the differential impacts of assessments and evaluations (including tests) on a fictitious student.

Painted with a variety of brushstrokes, Parts 2 and 3 depict central aspects of educational legacies in two former empires. Both parts illustrate some central impacts on students regarding the evolution of respective school assessments and evaluations. Emphases are on the Chinese and, as importantly, the British colonial models of education. Some interesting shared commonalities are highlighted in the emerging discussion. One notes that the British Empire covered much of the earth's land mass until it was dismantled gradually after World War II. A constant visible yet understated reminder of the power of empire was once depicted graphically in many schools. On large Mercator world maps, bright pink or red colors detailed the immense, global distribution of British dominions, colonies, and protectorates. Often, the world maps were hung on the walls at the front of our classrooms, adjacent to the chalkboards, as silent representations of power. Each author, Kim Koh, originally from multilingual (e.g., Malay, Chinese dialects, Mandarin, Tamil, and English) Malaysia, Sean Steel from English- and French-speaking Canada, and Cecille DePass, from the English-speaking Caribbean, has been influenced in different ways and times, directly and/or indirectly, by the British Empire and its colonial model of education. Part 3 of this chapter draws on my lived educational experiences by sharing a few personal narratives which largely complement the literature discussed in Part 2.

In Part 4, the discussion shifts considerably to explore issues of transferability of one's educational credentials, from the south to the north. The pictures highlight ways in which life chances of cue-conscious and cue-assertive learners (Meighan, 1986) who have excelled and gained university qualifications in their respective countries of origin are often denied opportunities to enter the Canadian high education segment of the labor market (Carnoy, 1980; DePass, 1988). A few vignettes from the Alberta Network of Immigrant Women (ANIW, 2015) question notions of universality and transferability of formal educational qualifications obtained in countries of origin, specifically in countries other than the US, Britain, Western Europe, or members of the old British Commonwealth (Canada, Australia, New Zealand, and South Africa). Part 4 demonstrates that devaluation of educational credentials is not a deliberate, intentional act by gatekeepers/administrators or employers. Unintentionally, and paradoxically, because of systemic biases in formal assessment procedures and processes, the Canadian state loses the benefits of immigrants' knowledge, expertise, skills and indeed, billions of dollars in taxes, from sizable numbers of immigrant professionals who are, at best, underemployed (ANIW, 2015; Burke, 2016; DePass, 1988; Guo, 2007; Hawthorne, 2007; Kelly et al., 2014; World Education Services, Forum, n.d.).

In concluding, the chapter positions the discussion of assessment and evaluation within a broader context of the United Nations (UN) and the United Nations Educational, Scientific, and Cultural Organization's (UNESCO) aspirations of achieving a fairer, more equitable world in which access to education is no longer a dream for most of the world's children and adults, in particular, girls and women.

Part 1: Illustrations of Multiple Perspectives

Pictures in the First Fable: The Many-Sidedness of Things: The Blind Men and the Elephant[1]

Once upon a time, a raja told a trusted servant to gather all the blind men in Savatthi and "show" them a mature elephant. The servant did as commanded. He gathered together the men who were born blind and brought them to stand around a magnificent elephant. He said loudly to the group, "This is an elephant." To the first blind man, he said, "Here is an elephant" and then guided the blind man to use his sensitive fingers to feel a small section of the elephant's head.

He allowed the second man to touch one of the elephant's ears; the third patted a tusk, and another felt the trunk. Each of the others touched a foot, the elephant's back, the tail, and finally, the tuft of the tail. The servant repeated firmly, "This is an elephant" as he guided each blind man to feel with his fingers a specific, predetermined part of the elephant's body.

The raja then questioned each blind man individually. "Have you seen the elephant? Tell me; what is it?" Each man replied in the affirmative, yet, the raja noted that as he listened, the responses were significantly different. The blind man presented with the head, stated, for example, that the elephant was like a pot. The man "shown" an ear announced that it was like "a winnowing basket." The man who felt the tusk contradicted, stating, "It is like plowshares." Another who touched the trunk declared, "It is like a plow." Each man had a different tactile experience of the elephant and accordingly gave a different explanation and interpretation based on prior knowledge and life experiences. The elephant's body was a grain silo; "the foot, a pillar; the back, a mortar; the tail, a pestle; the tail's tuft, a brush" (Wang, 1995).

Hearing such different interpretations of the same phenomenon, the men argued vehemently and fell to fighting among themselves.

The raja was delighted.

Pictures in the Second Fable: Feasting on Goodies in the Educational Cornucopia: The King and the Bird[2]

Long, long, ago, in a faraway land, there once lived a king who was much loved and known for his just, equitable, respectful, and peaceful rule of the country. One day, one of his most trusted advisors, the minister of education, brought a problem to the king's attention; it was likely to have serious repercussions throughout the land. He reported that despite the best efforts of the policymakers and practitioners of his ministry, the bird, called the learner or student, was ailing. When pressed with more questions, the minister admitted that the bird appeared to be gravely ill. They had tried everything, he said, but the bird's health continued to decline.

In response, the king gathered all the gurus with doctoral degrees in the field of educational assessments and evaluations. The doctors were highly respected for their knowledge of the best models, theories, and applications in the field. He sought their advice.

In respectful tones, some gurus recommended assessments based on behavioral models of education. Senior gurus recommended caution; they advised sticking with tried and true methods, which had existed for thousands of years, in which tests relied on memorization and rote learning of secular and sectarian knowledge. A few advocated teaching to the test itself using canonical sources. Others endorsed a back-to-basics approach. A number of gurus supported versions of Bloom's taxonomy to test students' higher-order abilities and thinking skills. Another group suggested that Socratic methods of questioning and critical thinking were still applicable. Still others advocated constructivist methods. Some recommended experiential learning and assessment, while others wished to rely on innovative methods using advanced technologies for teaching, learning, and testing.

The king was impressed. He proclaimed that all the gurus' recommendations should be compiled in a massive tome he would sanction. Furthermore, he stated that all approaches and methods of teaching and assessment should be implemented during the next three to five years. Also, all the methods were to be evaluated to determine their respective merits.

Time passed. The bird was fed each method or approach as a steady diet–sometimes, sequentially–other times, concurrently. Sometimes the bird was fed with an approach that proceeded through stages with re-iterative feedback and feed-forward systems loops of diagnostic, formative, and summative assessments.

At times, the bird responded well, growing fatter and fatter; however, over time, the bird became increasingly bloated. Most of the time, the bird was so stuffed with educational goodies in the teaching, learning, and assessment cornucopia that it steadily became sicker. It stopped warbling its cheerful songs in lyrical notes and subtle tones. The bird stopped imitating the voices of the humans who cared for it. After singing and performing for one specific, high-stakes summative assessment, the bird lay completely exhausted.

Eventually, the minister of education and his policymakers and practitioners realized the bird was dying. Despite their knowledge, best efforts, and good intentions, the bird lay in its cage, seldom moving. It refused to eat any more of the delicious goodies in the educational cornucopia. Highly perturbed, the minister reported to the king.

The king consulted with the minister of education and his wise advisors. The minister suggested they consult a wise woman, an elder. The king summoned the wise woman to his court and asked her advice. The woman looked carefully at the bird lying in the bottom of the cage.

Cautiously, she took the bird from its cage. Placing it gently in the king's hands, she faced the king, and said, softly, "My lord, the future of the bird and education in this country lies in your hands."

Part 2: Portraits of Education and Assessments

Part 2 explores some of the history, assumptions, characteristics, and impacts of different types of formal assessments and evaluations. First, I summarize students' responses to schooling and assessment in Western contexts. Second, Part 2 highlights a few paintings of education in China, once a major civilization with its extensive Asian empire and currently, a significant economic power with the potential to become a significant player in international higher education, especially for students from the southern hemisphere. Third, I paint pictures of education and assessment in a few countries which were part of the British Empire. In particular, this discussion maps positive and negative impacts of assessments on learners or students who have become strategists, labeled, respectively, as being cue-conscious, cue-assertive, or cue-deaf (Meighan, 1986; Miller & Parlett, 1983).

From research in Western contexts, *cue-conscious* learners portray specific abilities and characteristics such as discovering explicit and implicit ways examinations function and determining stated and unstated performance requirements and benchmarks for success or failure (Davies, 1986; Meighan, 1986). Cue-conscious learners, for example, identify:
– assignments that "really count;"
– specific types of presentations (oral and/or written) likely to produce the highest grades; and,
– important cues and clues concerning upcoming summative examinations.

In addition, if tests or examinations are internally assessed, cue-conscious learners find out the specializations, preferences, and perspectives of instructors who are likely to grade the tests or examinations. Interestingly, cue-conscious learners learn the explicit, formal, and tacit hidden curricula, although the latter was not officially presented in classes (Meighan, 1986; Samuel, 2003).

Some are more *assertive learners* (Davies, 1986; Meighan, 1986). Besides acquiring the characteristics of cue-conscious learners, they take the process further, specifically with regards to upcoming examinations and examiners involved. Cue-assertive learners, for example:
– systematically prepare for examinations well in advance;
– probe instructors with specific questions about the upcoming examinations;
– read relevant and recently published literature in the field; and
– read a sample of specific external/internal examiners' and instructors' publications to determine examiners' academic and research interests.

Such students have mastered their respective fields of study. Furthermore, they hone effective communication strategies which deliberately create the best impressions in their oral and written examination performances. To quote an examiner, during the follow-up discussion to determine whether a doctoral student passed her candidacy or comprehensive examination in education, "Ms. Angela Jones [pseudonym] has very strong potential. She knows the literature, writes well, and is extremely articulate" (Memory candidacy exam early 2010s. I was the Ph.D. student's supervisor and mentor).

Depending on examiners' and instructors' previous roles and experience with teaching, learning, and assessment, they may distinguish even more between the characteristics of cue-assertive and cue-aggressive learners. Using my personal experiences and observations as a professor and instructor of graduate and preservice teachers at a Canadian university, the boundaries between the two groups of learners are likely to overlap and are influenced by the examination's significance. In major examinations, some cue-assertive learners may present aggressive behaviors ranging from denial to confrontation. Such behaviors are possible if students are challenged to go beyond their respective "comfort zones," for example, when students are invited, in some graduate courses, to re-examine the foundations and evolutions of their respective disciplines.

In contrast, *cue-deaf* learners live in their own world and are inattentive to explicit or implicit cues. Some remain unaware. Some function at naive levels of consciousness (Freire, 1982). Some care little about compulsory schooling and higher education. Whatever the reason, all disregard instructors' cues and clues about the forthcoming examinations. In doing so, the hidden curriculum, underpinning schooling, and examinations remain intact. On the one hand, one remembers that Albert Einstein, Thomas Edison, Winston Churchill, and other famous individuals were once labeled as cue-deaf learners. Supposedly, they were unlikely to become either high academic achievers or succeed in the adult world.

On the other hand, another interpretation from a dialectic (conflict) perspective is that schooling, assessment, and testing processes, procedures, and mechanisms serve predominantly, middle-class interests. Accordingly, teenaged girls, students from working-class homes, and disadvantaged ethnic, racial, or religious groups are really not all cue deaf. They know how the systems function. In response, some refuse, underachieve, or drop out; others contest and, in so doing, disrupt established patterns of dominance and oppression associated with education and assessment in several countries.

Pictures of Education and Standardized Examinations in China

In this section, the pictures highlight the evolution of education and examinations in Mainland China. Thousands of years ago, China developed one of the earliest and most rigorous summative examination system for male students. At that time, every male student in every village, even students from poor rural regions, could take the examinations (personal communication, Leith Lowe, June 5, 2017). After studying for many years, a few students became public officials. By 2200 BC, the Emperor continued the process of assessments. He even had his bureaucrats formally examined every third year to determine whether and to what extent they could hold their respective offices (Gregory, 2004).[3]

During the Han dynasty (206 BC-AD 220), for the Imperial Examination, or Keju, applicants or prospective mandarins were examined in five subjects deemed significant to the empire's effective functioning (Ash, 2016; Gregory, 2004): civil law, military affairs, agriculture, revenue, and geography. The Keju examination remained the sole criterion for selection of bureaucrats from the seventh century until its abolition in 1905 (Ash, 2016). A thematic essay, the "eight-legged paper," required argumentation in eight sections. Candidates were required to quote from the classics, from Confucius and Mencius (Ash, 2016). By 1370, due to the dominance and pervasiveness of Confucian thinking, the examination became grueling. It was written over three days, during which time the candidates wrote and lived in isolation. According to Ash, applicants were confined to a single cell. Only 1% of applicants eventually passed the examination to become mandarins (Ash, 2016; Gregory, 2004). For a deeper discussion, see S. Guo (2005).

Yansheng Guo (2008) and Shibao Guo (1996, 2005, 2008) meticulously trace the major changes in education, evaluation, and teacher training in China during the 20th century. They document central aspects of Confucian education, the Imperial Examination, and the authoritarianism and elitism embedded in notions that knowledge is "poured into" empty, passive vessels (Guo, 2008). Interestingly, notions of students being empty vessels, clean slates, as well as strictures to students to "leave your home culture at the door" are associated historically and comparatively with schooling in Western and Northern countries. In countries such as Canada and the US, public schooling often regarded students as empty vessels whose home cultures were left at the door. Accordingly, public schooling has been an influential force for assimilating or integrating children from cultures other than the mainstream, such as immigrant and indigenous children.

Yansheng Guo (2008) and Shibao Guo (2008) summarize John Dewey's pragmatic education, which significantly influenced educational philosophy from the 1920s to the rise of Mao's People's Republic. As important, Y. Guo notes the contributions of Mocall's psychological and evaluation tools adopted in elementary and secondary schools. S. Guo identifies the significant influences of the Soviet model. Regarding recent changes, S. Guo argues that because of economic globalization, education is oriented toward global competition and a market mentality (more detailed analyses are presented by Guo & Guo, 2016). Furthermore, evidence of the central state control of education is demonstrated, for example, in evaluation mechanisms, fierce competition for limited spaces in higher education, and a written examination approach to teaching (e.g., Guo, 2008; Guo, 2016).

The current examination, the Gāokǎo, was introduced in 1952. It is regarded as a "distant relation of the Keju." It was suspended during the Cultural Revolution and re-introduced after Mao's death (Ash, 2016). At present, the examination includes four, three-hour papers: Chinese, English, mathematics, and a choice from either the natural sciences or humanities. The questions remain extremely difficult. "The math examination, for example, has been compared with a university level course in Britain" (Ash, 2016). From the students' perspectives, the most challenging component is the essay examination. In 2015 for example, the essay examination prompts included the following: "Do butterfly wings have colors?" and "Who do you admire the most: A biotechnology researcher, a welding engineering technician, or a photographer?" In 2016, the choice was between, "old accent" or "mysterious bookmark" (Ash, 2016).

However, despite significant political and economic changes in the latter part of the 20th century, Confucius' influence appears to linger. In North America, Huang and Klinger's (2006) study documents the perspectives of four Chinese university graduate students who completed their bachelor's degrees in Chinese universities and enrolled later in US and Canadian universities. Interestingly, the researchers trace the longevity of Confucius' philosophy of education in the graduate students. Although the sample is small, they argue that Confucius' influence is evident in notions of effortful and respectful learning, behavioral reform, and the pragmatic acquisition of essential knowledge. Essentially supporting Tweed and Lehman's (2002) research, Huang and Klinger emphasize the "effort-focused conceptions of learning, pragmatic orientations to learning, and acceptance of behavioral reform as an academic goal" (Tweed & Lehman, 2002, p. 93 in Huang & Klinger, 2006, p. 49. For a fuller discussion, see, Huang & Klinger, pp. 49–52).

Interestingly enough, despite the positive and negative influences of revolutions in 20th-century China, Confucian values are still evident in the society's deep structures and remain engrained in "… Chinese people's viewpoints, ways of thinking, behaviors and experiences" (Huang & Klinger, 2006, p. 49). Unsurprisingly, students attribute academic successes to "hard work rather than ability" (Huang & Klinger, 2006, p. 49). In teaching a few mainland Chinese international, graduate students at a Canadian Prairie university from the mid-1990s to the early 2000s, I noted similar perspectives and attitudes to those identified in Huang and Klinger's (2006) qualitative study.[4]

The Chinese examination system has been criticized on several counts. Continuing acceptance results from the massive numbers of students enrolled in schools who take the examinations. Understandably, with intense competition, the examination's screening mechanism is supported to ensure that exceptional students can "trickle up" from poorer socioeconomic, minority cultural, and tribal backgrounds. Yan Guo's (2016) qualitative study of Chinese teachers reveals major critiques from the English teachers. Preparation for written examinations begins in grade seven for the grade nine examinations, and preparation for the grade 12 school leaving examinations begins from grade 10. For students who wish to enter the ivy league university in Beijing, the stress is incredible. One teacher, in discussing teaching and learning approaches, stated that instead of fostering communication skills, teachers are required to prepare students for written examinations. Further, if the emphasis shifts to fostering communication skills, the students are unlikely to pass the written examinations. Due to the system's authoritarianism, if students fail examinations, severe criticism is launched at the individuals involved, from the directors of the school boards through to the teachers themselves (Guo, 2016).

In response, some of the affluent parents have found alternatives for their children. They include sending them, first, abroad to study (Ash, 2016), or, second, to specific schools in China which offer, for example, provincial Canadian or Australian high school curricula and diplomas (personal communications from Bing Wang, Liaoning Normal University, Dalian, July, 2001; Thomas Patten, Euro-Canadian school principal, of a "Maple Leaf" school, Dalian, 2005; Keith Lowe, July, 2017). A third option involves transferring them, before the grade 12 examination, from a province with a much larger population and accordingly, far fiercer competition, to schools in provinces with smaller populations, e.g., Inner Mongolia (Ash, 2016).

Negative impacts of stress are attributed to the formidable examination system. Understandably, students create their own responses to the intense coaching and heavy school workloads which began in their early schooling (Ash, 2016; Guo, 2016). Some students develop a wide range of cheating strategies; some suffer nervous collapse, and unfortunately, some even commit suicide (Ash, 2016). Such negative responses to intense competition and examinations that determine one's life chances are not restricted to China. Some academics and educators, by deliberately developing and systematically exploring alternatives (in philosophical, theoretical, conceptual, policy, and practical terms) have created more humane forms of assessments such as authentic assessment and formative assessment or assessment for learning, which Kim Koh presents in her chapters of this book. I turn now to assessments and evaluations in another former empire.

Pictures of Assimilation: Education and Assessments in the Former British Empire[5]

The British colonial model of education, with its concomitant values, ideologies, assumptions, implications, and influences, has lasted for over 300 years in the English-speaking Caribbean, and from the mid- to late-nineteenth century in Sierra Leone, West Africa. Articles by Norel London (1991, 1996), Deo Poonwassie (1991), Handel Wright (1993), and Cecille DePass (2006, 2008) explore the impacts of colonization on students' formal educational opportunities and future life chances within highly structured social, cultural and economic systems.

London's (1996) analysis of education in Trinidad (1938–1955) draws on the language of quality control. The concept reminds us of F. W. Taylor's time and motion studies of factory workers in the US (Shepard, 2000). Today, the concept and practice of quality control have expanded considerably. Contemporarily, quality control includes continuous monitoring and evaluation of the production and distribution of manufactured goods and monitoring and assessing customer services and consumer satisfaction levels in sectors ranging from banking and commerce to retail and fast food industries, and increasingly, to faculty, instructors and staff in secondary and post-secondary educational institutions. In quite a few ways, today's quality control, assessment, and evaluation procedures, when applied to professors and instructors in some universities, appear similar to the Chinese emperor's periodic assessments of his mandarins and to employees who have to meet specified performance and productivity goals, objectives, and quotas in their respective organizations.

London's (1996) study of elementary school students concentrates on external inspectors' assessments and reports. He argues convincingly that a colonial education socializes British subjects to accept the existing social and economic hierarchies of the empire. Such an education ensures that most students become manual laborers (Brown, 2005; Poonwassie, 1991). As importantly, students learn to accept the hegemony and ruling groups' "inherent right to maintain their positions of dominance because they were culturally and even intellectually superior" (Bacchus, 1986, p. 21 in London, 1996, p. 46).

In such societies, testing and evaluation procedures are developed by gatekeepers to facilitate a gradual process of social change. Due to the types of formal and informal assessments and examinations implemented, some students trickle up in school systems. When examined, in light of Meighan's (1983) analysis, cue-conscious and cue-assertive learners are most likely to achieve success and trickle up. Cue-deaf learners remain oblivious; some drop out, and others "cool out." Most are forced to accept or create jobs in other emerging formal and informal economic sectors.

Some cue-conscious and cue-assertive students acquire the abilities and skills needed to pass different forms of compulsory, standardized examinations. Understandably, more middle-class students than working-class students are likely to succeed in such schools, a similar pattern to that identified in China by Ash (2016). Admittedly, some individuals from the working classes who adopt education as a form of social mobility might one day become, for example, school teachers, religious ministers, clerks, and low-level administrators in the public service. Some, in turn, become the next generation of gatekeepers, themselves guarding the doors to education and occupational and career mobility. Thus, educational successes are measured mainly in terms of one's ability to conform to the norms and expectations of the school systems, perform exceptionally well in competitive examinations, and become assimilated within colonial, occupational, and career hierarchies.

London's article, mentioned earlier, is based on an analysis and interpretation of written reports produced by external school inspectors who examined elementary school students. Given the school inspectors' structural, functional, and conceptual perspectives, their evaluations of student's abilities, recorded in school logs, are congruent with the model of teaching basic skills and instituting screening procedures for selecting low-level functionaries.

Based on oral and written examinations, observations, and careful scrutiny of students' performances under examination conditions, specific inspectors' comments are insightful. Such comments include weak arithmetic; more practice in school English is required to reduce negative home influences; poetry is taught to appreciate the beauty of the English heritage; school gardens are established to inculcate manual labor skills (Brown, 2005; Poonwassie, 1991); and finally, school discipline is poor (London, 1996). In light of the critique of school discipline, it is important to note that most elementary, government schools in the English-speaking Caribbean were, and still are, basic, one-room structures with open sides. The classes are divided by portable blackboards. Generally, most of the schools are overcrowded, understaffed, and many lack even basic resources. I suspect similar types of schools exist throughout the Southern Hemisphere. A cautionary note, however: impressive school structures and human, physical, material, and high-tech resources are not necessarily synonymous with excellence in teaching and learning.

London astutely asserts that generally, school inspectors record schools' and, by extension, students' failings. Schools' roles in a colonial society are primarily to encourage cultural assimilation and "acceptance of the preferred canons of speaking and behavior that would hopefully be firmly entrenched long after the dismantling of the colonial regime" (London, 1996, p. 55). In language far more graphic than London's, Austin Clarke's (2005) memoir describes his elementary and secondary schooling. By winning a government scholarship, Clarke left a working-class elementary school with a brutal headmaster to attend one of the prestigious boy's secondary schools on the island. He stresses the significance of the Senior Cambridge Examinations (overseas) in terms of shaping students' life chances.

The Cambridge examinations represented the quintessential schooling-leaving examination in the British colonies. Clarke writes of the Cambridge examinations at the end of his secondary schooling as follows:

> The examination papers were sent to Barbados by English post and were kept sealed somewhere in the Ministry of Education until that frightening day when they were opened [by external invigilators] with great caution, determination and fuss.
>
> The questions to which the students wrote responses ... had nothing to do with the way we lived, with the way we understood ourselves ... [the examinations could determine] whether ... we were going to get into the Civil Service ... to the "Col-Sec's" [Colonial Secretary's] Office and rise to positions of power and hold confidential files ... perhaps to be given an OBE at age 50, with one foot in the grave ... [It] determined whether we were going to languish and starve on small salaries as elementary school teachers[It] determined whether one became an overseer on a sugar plantation.
>
> ... whether one would ... go to England ... enter the Inns of Court ... study law ... whether we would enter a British University ... It meant life and could mean death. (Clarke, 2005, pp. 211–212)

As in Barbados, Poonwassie's (1991) article demonstrates that in Guyana, another former British colony, education follows the British colonial educational model and is highly centralized. Accordingly, most major decisions are made by the Minister of Education and staff in the capitol. Understandably, since education functions in conservative ways in, for example, Guyana, Jamaica, and Trinidad, the British examinations are given more legitimacy and impact one's career and life chances. Poonwassie argues:

> The prestige, power and opportunity accorded to these certificates were paramount in the minds of parents and students ... if one ever wanted to become a medical doctor or a lawyer (the two prized professions), the A-level certificate was a basic requirement. (Poonwassie, 1991, p. 49)

Across the Atlantic, in another former British colony, Sierra Leone, West Africa, a similar trend is noted. There, attachments to the Cambridge examinations, as in the English-speaking Caribbean, continued well after political independence. Handel Wright's paper (1993), for example, shows that strong affinities with the British Advanced Level examinations still exist among high school students in Sierra Leone, despite the realization that A-level subjects do not pertain to their future careers (Wright, 1993). A few students state that only one Sierra Leonean author's work has been assigned as a literature school text. Whether intentionally or unintentionally, students receive the hidden message that Sierra Leonean literature is neither worthy of serious study (Wright, 1993) nor important enough to be assessed in formal examinations. Essentially, omitting Sierra Leonean texts from the formal literature school curriculum represents another form of the hidden curriculum. Wright suggests that poor performance in the advanced literature examination should be considered within the larger context of the type of literature taught and punishments given for speaking one's mother tongue (Wright, 1993). Although discussing school students of the 1990s in Sierra Leone, Wright's study supports key aspects of London's, Poonwassie's, Clarke's, and Brown's studies concerning assessments and evaluations in the former British West Indies.

London's (1996) analyses of school inspectors' reports demonstrate that evaluation has long been a central component of the practice of schooling. Raised and educated in the British West Indies, London could have perhaps enhanced his argument from a more explicit Caribbean historical perspective. A colonial education in the West Indies has a well-established historical mission, namely the spread of Christianity, acquisition of basic literacy and numeracy skills, production of a compliant, deferential labor force, and maintenance of a social and economic structure associated with a plantation society (Brown, 2005; Moore & Johnson, 2004; Poonwassie, 1991).

Perhaps too, London has overstated his claim that imperial representatives, in this case, school inspectors and examiners, anticipated the dissolution of the empire. It is unlikely that the end of the empire was a conventional notion. The empire's entrenchment in the post-colonial era is reflected in some of the key characteristics of a colonial educational model continued well into the late 1970s. They include instructional pedagogies, syllabuses, texts, screening and examination procedures to enter traditional and comprehensive secondary schools, and school leaving examination systems. It is possible that London's personal experiences underpin his claims concerning the enduring aspects of a colonial education. The effects of a colonial education, such as devaluation, dismissal, and denial of one's heritage, language and culture, and assimilation into the dominant colonial culture, remain hot topics for debate (e.g., personal notes, from a Maori development seminar, Victoria University of Wellington, August 2006 and presentations by three First Nations, University of Alberta doctoral students at the Comparative and International Education Society of Education Preconference, University of Calgary, May, 2016).

In the Caribbean and several other countries once part of the British Empire, neither schools nor churches were monolithic, total institutions; they unintentionally fostered resistance in fields ranging from politics through to the humanities, social sciences and the arts. In the English-speaking Caribbean, extreme resistance was/is demonstrated, for example, in the political arena by Norman and Michael Manley, Eric Williams, Ralph Gonzales; in literature by Derek Walcott, CLR James, Mervyn Morris, Cecil Gray, Edward Baugh, Kamu Braithwaite, Pamela Mordecai; in history by Douglas Hall, Elsa Goveia, Lucille Mathurin-Mair, Sir Hilary Beckles, Brain Moore and Verene Shepherd; in the social sciences by Walter Rodney and Brain Meeks, to name a few of the well-known academics; in the arts by Derek Walcott, Edna Manley, Trevor Rhone, Bob Marley, and Louise Bennett. Most excelled in colonial schools and later, universities either in the north or at the University of the West Indies (UWI).

There are signs of major changes in post-colonial education. In the English-speaking Caribbean, progressively, since the late 1950s to early 1960s, the inclusion of works by Caribbean authors has assumed more significance in the curricula and examination syllabuses. In fact, by 1964, the Cambridge O-level and A-level examination papers included regional content in history and geography. Yet, in Jamaica, for instance, by the mid- to late-1960s, not all secondary school students who took the Cambridge O-level and A-level examinations were taught Caribbean history and/or geography for examination purposes (As I learned from discussion with several friends and relatives and when I went to the UWI, in fall, 1967).

Toward the end of the 20th and in the first few decades of the 21st century, the inclusion of national and regional contexts, content, and perspectives for instance, in school curricula and examination syllabuses in social sciences, humanities, and arts, has become commonplace. In some cases, I suspect that the curricula have adopted transformational as well as additive models of curriculum and examination reform. For examples of curriculum reform, see N. Sheldon, n.d. and Caribbean Examinations Council (CXC, Gordon, 1983). Furthermore, a number of Caribbean educators have produced school texts for the Commonwealth Caribbean which are usually targeted to prepare students for high-stakes examination purposes.[6] It serves only accountability demands.

With a history of over 30 years, the CXC has successfully established itself as the premier examination body in the English-speaking Caribbean. Offering equivalency to the British General Certificate of Secondary Education, CXC assesses candidates in a wide range of 33 subjects including several Western-European languages, the humanities, agricultural and natural sciences, visual and theatre arts, business, industrial technology, and mechanical engineering (see www.cxc.org for web pages with lists of syllabuses, samples of past examination papers, current examination schedules, and texts).

With significant movements between countries of international students, academics, professionally educated immigrants, and refugees, and with the development and dissemination of information from knowledge economies, at times with instantaneous exchanges of ideas, virtual goods, and services between the north and south, facilitated by high-tech communications industries, I suggest that explorations of key issues mentioned in Part 2 should become central to the types of educational policies, assessments, and evaluation procedures deliberately implemented in present and future schools, universities and testing syndicates, in the north, south, east and west (Alexander, Osborne, & Phillips, 2000). The dilemmas associated with moving to any of the poles on the assessment and evaluation continuum are well presented by, for example, Allan Pitman's and Farrukh A. Chishtie's (2004) cogent analysis of education and examinations in sectarian Pakistan. As important are Shibao Guo's (1996, 2005, 2008, 2016) and Yan Guo's (2016) meticulous documentation of ideological shifts, implications, and impacts regarding Chinese education, teacher preparation, and adult learning/education.

My Story: Selected Vignettes

By the mid-20th century in the Caribbean, specifically, in Jamaica, the education system remained similar to that discussed earlier by London, Wright, and Poonwassie. I sat for the compulsory Ministry of Education's Common Entrance Examination in 1959. As an invited, keynote speaker, I presented my memories of sitting for the Common Entrance examination at "Checkmark," an educators' conference in assessment and evaluation at Nipissing University, Ontario (1997). I described my experiences of our class being coached by the school's headmistress, my apprehensions and expectations concerning the formidable one-day examination in arithmetic, English (which included an essay and comprehension questions), and another examination paper I do not remember (DePass, 1997). Through a young Anglican girl's eyes, I was impressed that the examination was held in the massive auditorium of a huge secondary, Roman Catholic girl's school with a stately church on the same property. The invigilators were retired school teachers and Ministry of Education administrators (as I learned much later). Everything was strange. Everything was on a larger scale, for example, the vast size of the exam room and the large numbers of primary students taking an extremely competitive, high-stakes exam in the same room. For the entire day, everything was on a larger and more intense scale than that of everyday life at my small preparatory school. I knew neither the school (the exam site) nor the invigilators. To Austin Clarke's (2005) description of the determination and fuss of the invigilators as they distributed the examination papers and in solemn tones, laid down the examination's rules, I add (after being a post-secondary invigilator and examiner myself) the pomp, circumstance, and rituals associated with a proctored closed-book examination. Initially, I was intimidated by the process. However, as usually happens in some examinations, there was the thrill of demonstrating my knowledge and skills, so assiduously acquired (see also Ash, 2016; Brown, 2005; Davies, 1998 for discussions of examination conditions and students' adaptations and performance strategies).

I was delighted when the examination results were published in the national newspaper, and I realized that I had won a scholarship to one of the prestigious high schools (a new, small, grant-aided, girl's school, closely affiliated with the Anglican Church). It was located in a modern, well-staffed and well-equipped two-story building (designed for the tropics) on spacious, manicured grounds of a former great house, a relic of the plantation and slavery era. The great house housed the administrative offices, library, tuck shop, staff room, prefect's room, and sixth forms. The school complex had two additional buildings for the kindergarten and preparatory schools. Both were in large, modern houses. I knew that those attending kindergarten, then preparatory and still later, a small, secondary girl's school (for some 300 students) were given privileges and opportunities not shared by most Jamaican school students. Indeed, we, the daughters of parents from the entire range of socioeconomic classes, and from the color, race, ethnic, and religious continuum associated with the Caribbean, were extremely privileged. I knew that access to education was not a right or entitlement. Indeed, by the 1960s, the number of male and female students enrolled in similar schools throughout the country was quite low. (DePass, 2008; Figueroa, 1971; Miller, 1996).

Although I was schooled and coached to work within the colonial system of education, during the 1960s, I was part of a transitional generation. We were the generation expected to accept leadership and nation-building roles in an independent country (see also Brown, 2005). Accordingly, at school, we acquired the knowledge, skills, and attitudes required for active citizenship in a politically independent country. For my part, I accepted unquestioningly the hierarchical educational system which existed then and still does to a considerable extent. I hurried through the ranks of the 'A' stream for scholarship students, assuming leadership roles such as form captain, girl guide, patrol leader, and later, sub-prefect, then prefect, and head girl. I passed my Cambridge Ordinary

(O)-level and Advanced (A)-level examinations, and in 1967, entered the UWI, Mona Campus, Kingston, Jamaica, to study for a bachelor's degree. Within a structural, functional, conceptual, and analytical perspective, the external O-level and A-level examinations were effective mechanisms to screen, select, and place students either on the educational ladder, probably to attend university or enter public or private sector employment, at fairly low levels (discussed earlier). As Clarke has argued, passing or failing the external examinations could determine one's life chances.

Before immigrated to Canada, my university work (B.A., UWI) as a Commonwealth scholar studying for a M.A. (Victoria University of Wellington, New Zealand), completing a postgraduate diploma in education (UWI), and teaching at two secondary schools and a teacher's college, I accepted the educational assessments and evaluations in which I had been schooled and immersed. Indeed, by the mid-1970s, I was one of the educators who developed the final multiple-choice tests in geography for students leaving the government's comprehensive schools. I participated actively in external assessment teams (with examiners from other teacher colleges) for student teachers completing their final, written, and practicum examinations. I was also an active member of the Jamaica team's preliminary discussions regarding the shift to the creation of a Caribbean Examination Certificate (CXC) in Geography for high schools. The regional examination was planned to gradually replace the Cambridge O-level examination in Geography.

Part 3: Re-Examining Cherished Notions of Assessment and Evaluation: A Memory

I turn now to pictures of a few of my graduate experiences at the University of Calgary after my migration to Canada in the mid-1980s. These caused me to reconsider my taken-for-granted notions of standardized examinations (i.e., high-stakes tests) I had experienced as a student and in turn, practiced in my teaching career in Jamaica during the 1970s. In fall 1984, I entered the graduate program in educational policy and administration studies, and four years later completed a Ph.D. in comparative and international education.

Dr. Rosa Garcia's (pseudonym) course in qualitative research methods consistently asked her graduate students a number of probing questions which, over time, challenged my easy acceptance concerning types of assessments and evaluations (e.g., standardized examinations, high-stakes tests, formative and summative assessments), which are removed from the lives of most undergraduate and graduate students in teacher education programs.

For Dr. Garcia's course, the prescribed textbook was by Thomas Green (1980). The text was the launching point from which Garcia summarized via lectures, for example, the evolution of philosophy in education and ways of analyzing rich information gathered in the field. Important for me, by adopting a multidisciplinary, intergenerational approach, Garcia invited us to critique articles published by a few of the department's professors. In doing so, Garcia introduced us to multiple perspectives within conservative, structural-functional, theoretical, and conceptual frameworks.

In several follow-up, one-on-one discussions with her, I explained in detail why I believed in, valued, and applied quantitative research methods to my post-secondary teaching in Jamaica, my master's research (economic geography), and urban planning research conducted in parts of Western Canada.

As an analytical philosopher and former social scientist, Dr. Garcia listened carefully. She usually responded in a quiet voice, with a twinkle in her eyes. Here is a compilation of some of her thought-provoking questions:

> Cecille, why do you think statistics measure everything? Have you thought that we use language and symbols, human constructs, to try to measure, test, compare, and evaluate, and present our findings in observable, measurable terms? Have you thought that the words we use in measuring and assessing are merely indicators? Can language measure that which is invisible? Have you thought that the questionnaires often discover information which tests the values of the questionnaires, and may not ask the more difficult, meaningful questions?

Like all of Dr. Garcia's lectures in philosophy and in follow-up discussions, her questions left me with serious reservations with which I grappled for a considerable period. Sean Steel's chapter in our book invites such conversations.

Many years passed before I realized the full impact of Dr. Garcia's qualitative research methods course. Indeed, for my dissertation and for several additional years, I continued to design and conduct surveys and highly quantitative research for the public and private sectors. For the most part, I unquestioningly accepted the education system and standardized examinations throughout my schooling. I accepted the universal examination syllabuses in secondary school subjects. I accepted the reliance on British texts in school and, to a large extent, in some university subjects. Accordingly, for me, developing the abilities to pass external examinations and achieving entry to and academic successes in three Commonwealth universities were all educational opportunities and privileges which provided continuing institutional assurances that my university qualifications were transferrable (DePass et al., 2017). In the next section, however, another cherished notion concerning transferability of university credentials is questioned and explored in a thought-provoking series of reflective paintings.

Part 4: Transferability of Academic Credentials: Assessments of Prospective Immigrant Professionals before and after Entering Canada

In Canada, prospective immigrant professionals are screened and assessed by federal government officials who use a point system.[7] The screening process was introduced in the late 1960s to establish which applicants are perceived as best-suited in terms of educational levels, formal training, proficiency in one of the two official languages (i.e., English and French), as well as immigration officers' general perceptions about the individual's abilities to fit the demands of the Canadian workplace. When the point system was introduced, immigration policies shifted from ascribed criteria, such as ethnicity and race to achieved criteria, such as education. Accordingly, educated and trained immigrants from the south, formerly denied entry, could migrate.

However, in their efforts to find jobs commensurate with their educational credentials and work experiences in their countries of origin, immigrants in Canada encounter several systemic hurdles. To be granted permission to practice in their specific fields, the immigrants' educational credentials are re-assessed by representatives of groups such as provincial, professional organizations and prospective employers.

Existing processes of accreditation used by professional associations in medicine, law, engineering, and teaching are based on the assessors' knowledge of post-secondary and secondary educational systems in Canada and overseas. In the evaluation of internationally trained professionals, knowledge of the equivalency and relative worth of university education and training are critical at the following points: assessment of educational qualifications, requirements for further education and examinations, and admission to internship and retraining programs. A World Education Services (WES) forum regarding the recognition of international credentials states that "Canadian employers lack the knowledge and experience" to assess such credentials (WES, citing research by Price Waterhouse, 1998). Furthermore, in some professions, employers use their discretion to assess university qualifications (WES, citing Riffel, 2006). Drawing extensively on research conducted in the mid-2000s, Kelly et al. (2014) analyze the negative impacts of the continuing failure to recognize the educational credentials of foreign-trained professionals.

From an immigrant perspective, entrance requirements for some professions in the high-education segment of the labor market (e.g., medicine, engineering, accounting, law, dentistry, architecture) are sometimes seen as too selective as well as based on hidden preferences and anachronisms. Minority immigrants focus on contradictions evident in criteria, policies, practices, and procedures used to assess formal educational credentials and training. They question the validity of the methods, criteria developed to assess foreign educational qualifications, and reluctance of representatives of organizations (in professional associations, corporate and public sectors) to change their methods of assessment, selection, and recruitment which are based on limited knowledge and stereotypes concerning the applicants' knowledge, skills, attitudes, and attributes.

For example, Joshua Thambiraj, M.D., who came originally from Malaysia, served as the then President of the Association of International Physicians and Surgeons of Ontario in 2007. The association consisted of 5, 000 foreign-trained medical doctors residing in Ontario. Dr. Thambiraj stated that he was unable to obtain his license as a pediatric surgeon during his first five years in Canada. Although he had passed the required Ontario medical exams, his credentials remained unrecognized (Dobrota, 2007).

Minority professionals contest existing assessment processes and procedures, arguing that they are inadequate and flawed. Some contend that assessment of foreign-trained professionals tends to be based on an implicit assumption, namely, that there is an international hierarchy of post-secondary educational systems. In such a hierarchy, Northern and Western universities are depicted in a more positive light than are universities in the East and South. Identifying the structural dilemma, Dr. Thambiraj, for example, states, "There is a kind of dissonance between acknowledging the problem and finding a solution" (quoted by Dobrota, 2007). Kamal Sehgal, M.S., director of the ANIW, summarizes the organization's continuing efforts, since 1999, to encourage Albertan professional associations in medicine, nursing, and dentistry to take action and remove artificial barriers which restrict entry to the respective professions (personal communiqué, April 28, 2017).

In contrast, defenders of existing methods of screening, assessment, and selection, who support a gradual, ameliorative process of change, if any, justify the existing policies and procedures to select applicants for admission to professional associations and for jobs in major corporate and public sector organizations for reasons which include the following:
– Very little is known of the education, assessment, and training of applicants from the South, in particular, applicants who are educated in their home countries and not in, e.g., Britain and the US.

- Costs of such thorough, well-considered assessments may outweigh possible benefits.
- Existing assessment methods ensure that, for the public good, standards are maintained, and thus, risks to professions, organizations and/or the public are minimized.

The impression of systemic biases which, on the one hand, favor some graduates with educational credentials, and on the other, exclude those with potentially equivalent credentials, is supported. Some professional associations grant preference to immigrants educated and trained in countries such as the US, Britain, and the older British Commonwealth countries (e.g., Australia, New Zealand). Stated reasons for such preference include that more is known of the university education and training in some Northern economically developed countries and far less is known about the university education in most other countries (see DePass, 1988, pp. 171–190 for lengthy discussion). Although DePass's (1988) study was completed some time ago, because it examines structural and systemic issues, not surprisingly, later research (e.g., Guo, 2007; Kelly et al., 2014) and information from the Alberta Network of Immigrant Women (ANIW) demonstrate that, to a great extent, systemic hurdles and deterrents immigrant professionals encounter are still alive and well.

Alberta Network for Immigrant Women Action Research Projects

In Alberta, over some 25 to 30 years, ANIW has conducted several qualitative action research projects. ANIW's research has explored the significant barriers to meaningful employment faced by international graduate, professional women. More recently, ANIW's research with immigrant medical graduates has concentrated on hurdles experienced by foreign-trained immigrant dentists. In the following vignettes,[8] a few immigrant dentists, in their own words, identify major problems that restrict or prohibit their ability to re-enter dentistry in Canada.

Vignette 1

I came to Canada in 2012 for my family to have greater opportunities than my home country could provide. Having worked in my country as a general dentist and having a thriving private practice, [it is ironic that] my qualifications are not recognized in Canada. For the last three years, I have been trying to pass my licensing examinations. So far, I have completed two of the five examinations.

As the years pass, your hands lose the skill, and there is no program that can help me to practice my skills, [so] passing the clinical examination will be very difficult. My savings and my family have helped me to pay for the expenses of the examination and to survive in Canada.

It is taking me a long time to complete the requirements because I also started to work as a volunteer translator, which paid me a small fee.

The process of acquiring my license has been very stressful and uncertain, not only for me but also for my family. I did not expect that the process to get my license will be such a lengthy and a costly one and that I would be so undervalued in Canada.

I know of friends who have reached their limits of being away from practicing their profession and having no income who are now looking for jobs as dentists in other countries (A.J., male dentist from Pakistan).

Vignette 2

I am working with seniors as a translator and companion who drives them to their doctor's appointments. Most of my clients are Russian Jewish seniors who do not have English language skills.

I came to Canada in 2011 as a qualified practicing pediatric dentist with the hope of practicing my profession. So far, the costly expense of paying for the examination has not enabled me to write my licensing examination. Canada needs us but does not provide any kind of support. I feel very alone in my professional development. For a short period of time, I had support from ANIW, and the online course was very helpful; but since the organization could not continue to deliver the program [due to cuts in funding], I have been on my own trying to study, working, and coping with the stresses of *not knowing if I will ever be able to practice my profession* (A.K., female dentist from the Ukraine).

Vignette 3

We arrived in Canada three years ago today. My husband and I are dentists (B.D.S. degrees) back in India. If we challenge our exams (in one shot), it will take us at least two years and around three years if I go back to school. This is just the time taken to clear them, plus the time it will take to apply and wait for the application to be approved.

I have cleared the National Dental Assisting Examining Board (NDAEB) examination, *I wrote this exam just as a backup since we have to be registered to even practice as a dental assistant here*. I am in the process of challenging my NDEB (National Dental Examining Board) exams now.

Financially, I am getting a temporary living allowance from the Immigrant Access Fund (IAF) so that I can concentrate my whole energy into these exams ... I was working full time in a survival job, but for two months I became part-time ... Today, I quit my job for a month so that I can focus my energy into the studies to write my examination.

I will be finding something in my field once my exam is over. Therefore, it is only a matter of a month with no financial aid. However, we also have some savings, and IAF has been kind to grant us a temporary living allowance for a couple of months, which is allowing us to survive.

The exam is definitely stressful. I have been making a lot of sacrifices for my exams. I have a 17-month-old baby. But I am very, very determined. The exams do take a toll on our mind, finances, body, relationships, and mostly, family! The only thing keeping me going is my family. My mother has been with us for the past eight months just supporting us ... [to give us time to do] our studies and taking care of my daughter. My husband is also in the same exam process, so we are like study partners. On that front, I am blessed.

I am sorry to say this, but so far, Canada has not met my academic expectations. I would really appreciate it if you also forward or mention it to the Canadian government. What I don't understand is why we have to undergo the same registration exam for a dental assistant examination. It's like we cannot work as anything in our field. There are very limited accelerated programs, no refresher courses for the clinical exam. How can one even think of entering their own field even as an assistant?

I love this country and the people. But it's not been an easy road. I will not give up until I reach where I want to be. I have heard if you want to change the system, you have to get into it first, and that's what I plan to do (R. G., female dentist from India).

The ANIW vignettes are a small sample of the poignant stories of sizable numbers of professional men and women who perhaps may never practice their professions in Canada. The problems encountered which lead to underemployment and sometimes, medical issues, are likely to have impacts on the immigrant professionals and their families. Their children, in particular, might question the need to achieve success in school when they see the effects of downward mobility and the resultant loss of socioeconomic and cultural status on their parents and themselves.

Conclusion

This chapter contributes several paintings, symbolic portraits and sketches of formal assessments and evaluations in some countries once the "center of the center" (Galtung, 1976) in political, socioeconomic, cultural, and military terms, as well as of some former colonies on the periphery. Specifically, the portraits concentrate on major complexities and impacts concomitant with education, formal assessments, and evaluations in several countries in the British Empire, a few countries in the British Commonwealth and the Western world, and the Chinese tradition. Tracing changes over time and considering personal vignettes enable us to question the easy acceptance of concepts such as universality, the structure and applicability of assessments, and the transferability or portability of educational credentials.

This discussion questions taken-for-granted assessment practices regarding high-stakes testing which significantly affect students' life opportunities. The supporting literature traces the evolution of examinations in China and some former British colonies. Further exploration of former colonies identifies issues of relevance and inclusion of local contexts and content in education and examinations. Perhaps the most troubling issue highlighted, however, is the recurrent Canadian dilemma regarding effective integration of immigrant professionals from the South and countries in Eastern Europe. For the most part, as indicated, for example, in 2015, vignettes from ANIW, as well as earlier research by DePass (1988) and Shibao Guo (2007), foreign university educational credentials and previous work experiences are not generally accepted by the high education segment of the Canadian labor market. This is quite ironic when one considers that many Southern university students, in particular those who study the natural sciences, often learn from the same university texts produced in England and the US, used by their counterparts in the north.

In light of the earlier discussion regarding types of learners, the internationally prepared professionals who become immigrants are likely to be cue-conscious and cue-assertive learners in their countries of origin. However, because of the hidden curriculum in Canada, they are effectively excluded from jobs for which they have been educated and trained. Such education and training, although recognized by immigration officials, ironically, are not recognized in comparable and equivalent employment sectors in Canada. That the immigrant professionals have been educated and trained in other countries at no cost to the Canadian taxpayers is another irony.

Economic developments of Western industrial and post-industrial societies, including Canada, tend to be linked with notions, expectations, and policies that the distribution of economic rewards such as education should be based on universalistic and individualistic principles of achievement and divorced from ascribed criteria. Further, Western perspectives about concepts of social development are closely coupled with notions of progress and human rights principles. Still further, such thinking underpins the international ranking of nation-states (for lengthy discussions, see Abdi & Guo, 2008; Berting, 1995; and the UN Universal Declaration of Human rights) as well as periodic international rankings of education (e.g., PISA, TIMSS) and access to schools for girls and boys (Organization for Economic Cooperation and Development [OECD] reports).

Undeniably, much progress has been made in improving access to education. There is widespread international acceptance of such universal concepts as access to public education, enshrined in the UN International Declaration of Human Rights (1948, quoted in the Appendix), and more recently, UNESCO's "Education for All" initiative (Dakar, 2000) has been sanctioned. International endorsements of subsequent UN conventions such as the Elimination of Racial Discrimination, also exist.

A few sentences from two of Hilary Clinton's addresses (1995 and 1997) concerning the larger international context are worth remembering and highlighting as challenges to all of us, researchers, educators, graduate students, and preservice teachers.

First, "If there is one message ... from this conference, let it be that human rights are women's rights and women's rights are human rights" (Fourth World Conference for Women, Beijing, 1995, quoted by Clinton, 2014, p. 561).

Secondly, Clinton echoes Eleanor Roosevelt, who said:

> We have not expanded the circle of human dignity far enough. There are still too many of our fellow men and women excluded from the fundamental rights proclaimed in the declaration, too many whom we have hardened our hearts against—those whose human suffering we fail fully to see, to hear, to feel ... The full enfranchisement of the rights of women is unfinished business in this turbulent century. (Opening address, Fiftieth Anniversary, Universal Declaration of Human Rights, 1997, UN Headquarters, New York, quoted by Clinton, 2014, p. 567)

Many countries still have a long, hard road to travel regarding human rights, women's rights, and equal access to education. In some countries, education remains a dreamed-of opportunity for the larger population, especially for girls and women. In contrast, in parts of the world where there is wide access to education, formal assessments and examinations challenge one's demonstrated strengths in terms of acquiring the prescribed knowledge, skills, and attitudes. Examinations evaluate content knowledge and communication skills. As importantly, they test one's performance and endurance. They assess whether one is able to meet and conquer the severity and rigidity of closed book and oral examinations. Admittedly, over time, in some North American universities, examination processes have expanded considerably to include written, take-home and open-book, and, in some universities, even open, public oral examinations (at the graduate level, due to access to technology, increasingly, final, doctoral oral examinations, tend to occur, in part, via Skype or telephone).

As educators, we can act like the dream catchers created by North American First Nations and become dream makers who continue to work collaboratively with our students in educational relationships as educators/educatees (Freire, 1972, 1982, 1987). Similar to receptive students, educators can be cue-aware and assertive in responding to changing educational and social circumstances where traditional means of assessment and evaluation may not meet current conditions. We can be critically conscious of the range and applicability of assessments confronted by our students. Likewise, it is significant for educators to realize that evaluation has a far-reaching impact on lives and employment of all students. As importantly, it can be seen to play a critical role in the success or failure of immigrants moving from the South to countries in the North.

Despite the turbulent times in which we live, we need to live with hope for a better future. We work to create teaching and learning environments in which formal education leads to freedom (Hooks, 1994) from ascribed criteria. As Dr. Garcia consistently challenged me to understand, for some questions, there are no easy answers, whether they appear phrased as multiple-choice, short answer, or essay.

Notes

1. Adapted, embellished, and expanded from Randy Wang's (Princeton, 1995) somewhat lengthier version. He attributes the fable to the Buddhist canon (Udana 68–69). Wang also indicates that some think that the fable's origins are Jainian. It illustrates "the many-sidedness of things."
2. A highly embellished memory of the fable. Since the mid-1990s, I have heard at least two versions of this fable and have included a third, by Susan Tobin, titled, "The Hermit and the Children" (Brody et al., 1992, p. 1), in some of my undergraduate and graduate classes at the University of Calgary. I first heard the fable from a young Latin American woman, a community leader, to demonstrate the need for meaningful collaboration between the youth leaders, organizers, and presenters at the Second International Conference for Young Leaders, Jeanne Suave Foundation, at McGill University, Montreal Quebec, in spring 1994. Second, Jagruti Dolakia (Ph.D., Psychology) presented her version at the Canadian Association for Curriculum Studies(CACS), Canadian Society for the Study of Education (CSSE) annual conference, 1994, University of Calgary. Dolakia stated that her version of the fable came from India.

3 Gregory explains the rigorous process of examinations, staged over many years, in which knowledge of Confucian thinking was predominant. In stage one, the examination was one day and one night. The candidate was placed in a small, isolated booth and wrote essays on assigned topics and a poem. Only 1 to 7% of the candidates passed the first exam. Several years later, enduring, progressively, more and more grueling exams, only a minute percentage eventually passed the exams and became mandarins.

4 In my university teaching experiences, (in education, University of Calgary), regarding teaching, co-supervising, and examining three Chinese graduate students (two Ph.D., one M.A.), further based on observations of a visiting lecturer from China who audited one of my graduate courses, and as a result of extensive discussions with Bing Wang, senior professor, Liaoning Normal University, Dalian (2001), I have noted that all three graduate students were determined to succeed and demonstrated the efficacy of hard work. To this end, they produced two comprehensive dissertations and a meticulous M.A. thesis, relied considerably on their supervisors and professors for guidance, and genuinely appeared to value education in extrinsic and intrinsic ways.

5 Selected parts of this section are based on my comparative education article (2006). Permission granted to include selected parts of information from the larger paper by M. Larsen, Editor, *Canadian and International Education*, fall 2016.

6 Understandably, after World War II, a sizable and increasing number of school texts with Caribbean emphases have been produced as a result of several factors such as the establishment of the UWI (initially affiliated with the University of London, and an autonomous institution since 1962), the emergence of a large number of highly educated Commonwealth Caribbean academics and educators (educated at home and abroad), the creation of politically independent nation-states, the emergence of regional publication companies and establishment of Caribbean arms of some British publishers, and further, the creation of the Caribbean Examinations Council. History, geography and social studies school texts include Roy Augier, Shirley Gordon et al.'s secondary history text (published from the 1960s), Graham Hart and Michael Morrissey's (1991), *Practical Skills in Caribbean Geography*, Books 1 &2, (Longman; Mike Morrissey's (2007), *Caribbean school atlas for Social Studies, Geography and History* (Harlow: Pearsons, Ed. Ltd/Longman); Michael Morrissey and David Barker's (1991), *Introducing Caribbean Geography. Vol. 1. A sense of place.* (Oxford University Press); Ruby King, Pam Morris et al.'s (2000/1983), *Social Studies through Discovery*. Kingston: Chalkboard Press; to name a few.

7 Assessment criteria for the immigration "point system" include "education and training, personal character, occupational demand, occupational skill, age, pre-arranged employment, knowledge of French and English, the presence of a relative

in Canada, employment opportunity in the area of destination" (Immigration regulations. Order in Council PC 1967–1616, 1967, Paragraph 3).

8 In March 2017, Kamal Sehgal (MSc), Director, ANIW, gave permission to include the vignettes (edited minimally).

References

Abdi, A. A., & Guo, S. (2008). *Education and social development: Global issues and analyses*. Rotterdam, The Netherlands: Sense Publishers.

Alexander, R., Osborn, M., & Phillips, D. (2000). *Learning from comparing: new directions in comparative educational research*. Oxford: Symposium Books.

Ash, A, (2016, November 11). China's terrible game of numbers. *Guardian Weekly*, pp. 26–30.

Augier, F. R., Gordon, S. C., Hall, D., & Reckford, M. (1983). *The making of the West Indies*. Burnt Mill: Longman Group Ltd.

Benjamin, A. (2014). *The impact of performance assessment on student's interest and academic performance in science* (Master's thesis). Retrieved from Uwispace.sta.uwi.edu/dspace/bitstream/handle/2139/39311/AvisBenjamin.pdf:sequence=

Berting, J. (1995). Patterns of exclusion: imaginaries of class, nation, ethnicity and gender in Europe. In J. N. Pieterse & B. Parekh (Eds.), *The decolonization of imagination* (pp. 149–166). London: Zed Books.

Book Project Collective. (Eds.). (2015). *Resilience and triumph: Immigrant women tell their stories*. Toronto: Second Story Press.

Brody, E., Goldspinner, J., Green, K., Leventhal, R., & Porcino, J. (1992). *Spinning tales weaving hope: Stories of peace, justice and the environment*. Philadelphia, PA: New Society Publishers.

Brown, Y. (2005). *Bodies, memories and empire: Life stories of growing-up in Jamaica: 1943–1965* (Doctoral thesis). University of British Columbia, Vancouver, BC, Canada.

Burke, H. (2016). The woman and her prize. *Cultural and Pedagogical Inquiry, 6*(2), 32–45.

Carnoy, M. (1980). Segmented labour markets in UNESCO. In *Education, work and employment* (Vol. 2). Paris: UNESCO.

Clarke, A. (2005). *Growing up stupid under the Union Jack: A memoir*. Toronto: Thomas Allen Publishers.

Dabrota, A. (2007, March 21). Immigrants upset over credentialing process. *Globe and Mail*, A4.

Davies, D. (1986). *Maximizing examination performance: A psychological approach*. London: Kogan Page Ltd.

Dei, G. J. S. (2000). Local knowledges and educational reforms in Ghana. *Canadian and International Education, 29*(1), 37–72.

DePass, C. (1997). *Beware the Jabberwok: An alternative perspective of standardized testing*. Keynote paper presented at the Checkmark Conference, University of Nipissing, Ontario.

DePass, C. (1988). *From periphery to periphery: Employment Equity for visible minorities in Canada* (Unpublished, Ph.D. dissertation, Department of Educational Policy and Administrative Studies). University of Calgary, Calgary.

DePass, C. (2006). Comparative education in changing times: Views with a southern exposure. *Canadian and International Education, 35*(2), 1–16.

DePass, C. (2008). 'Rock stone under river bottom …': Memories of a Caribbean childhood. In A. A. Abdi & G. Richardson (Eds.), *Decolonizing democratic education: Transdisciplinary dialogues* (pp. 151–160). Rotterdam, The Netherlands: Sense Publishers.

DePass, C., Lumsden, F., Jones, E., & Phillips, B. (2017). *The poetics of UWI, Geography* (Vol. 1). Tributes and Memories.

Dolakia, J. (1994). *The Raja and the bird*. Paper presented at the Canadian Association for Curriculum Studies Conference.

Dowrich, M. (2012). *Teacher perceptions of the implementation of the National Continuous Assessment Program in a primary school, St George East Education District, Trinidad and Tobago* (Master's thesis). The University of the West Indies, St Augustine Campus, St Augustine, Trinidad & Tobago. Retrieved from Uwispace.sta.uwi.edu/dspace/bitstream/handle/2139/12783/marvadowrich.pdf?sequence

Escoffery, G. (1989). Spring. In P. Mordecai (Ed.), *From our yard: Jamaican poetry since independence* (p. 6). Kingston: Institute of Jamaica Publications Ltd.

Figueroa, J. (1971). *Society schools and progress in the West Indies*. Oxford: Pergamon Press.

Flyvberg, B. (2001). *Making social science matter. Why social inquiry fails and how it can succeed again*. Cambridge: Cambridge University Press.

Freire, P. (1982). *Education for critical consciousness*. New York, NY: Continuum Publishing Corporation.

Freire, P. (1987/1972). *Pedagogy of the oppressed*. Harmondsworth: Penguin.

Galtung, J. (1976). A structural theory of imperialism. In W. Barclay, K. Kumar, & R. P. Simms (Eds.), *Racial conflict, discrimination and power: Historical and contemporary studies* (pp. 391–418). New York, NY: AMS Press Inc.

Ghosh, R., & Ray, D. (1991). *Social change and education in Canada*. Toronto: Harcourt Brace Jovanovich.

Gordon, S. C. (1983). *Caribbean generations: A CXC history source book*. New York, NY: Longman Group.

Green, T. F. (1980). *Predicting the behaviour of the educational system*. New York, NY: Syracuse University Press.

Gregory, R. J. (2014). *Psychological testing: History, principals and applications* (7th ed.). Boston, MA: Allyn & Bacon.

Guo, S. (1996). Adult teaching and learning in China. *Convergence, 29*(1), 21–33.

Guo, S. (2005). Exploring current issues in teacher education in China. *Alberta Journal of Educational Research, 51*(1), 69–84.

Guo, S. (2007).Tracing the roots of non-recognition of foreign credentials. In L. Hawthorne (Guest Ed.), *Foreign credential recognition* (Canadian Issues, Spring, pp. 36–38). Association for Canadian Studies.

Guo, S. (2008). China at the cross roads: Teacher education as a social development project. In A. A. Abdi & S. Guo (Eds.), *Education and social development: Global issues and analyses* (pp. 73–86). Rotterdam, The Netherlands: Sense Publishers.

Guo, Y. (2008). Translating western democratic education in the Chinese context. In A. A. Abdi & G. Richardson (Eds.), *Decolonizing democratic education: Transdisciplinary dialogues* (pp. 161–172). Rotterdam, The Netherlands: Sense Publishers.

Guo, Y. (2016). The impact of the market economy on English teachers. In S. Guo & Y. Guo (Eds.), *Spotlight on China: Changes in education under China's market economy* (pp. 119–136). Rotterdam, The Netherlands: Sense Publishers.

Hawthorne, L. (Guest Ed.). (2007). *Foreign credential recognition* (Canadian Issues, Spring). Association for Canadian Studies.

Huang, J., & Klinger, D. A. (2006). Chinese graduate students at North American universities: Learning challenges and coping strategies. *Canadian and International Education, 35*(2), 48–61.

Kelly, P., Marcelino, L., & Mulas, C. (2014). *Foreign credential recognition: Research synthesis, 2009–2013* (A CERIS report). Ottawa, ON: Citizenship and Immigration Canada. Retrieved from CERIS.ca/WP-content/uploads/2015/01/CERIS-Research-synthesis-on-foreign-credential-recognition

Lash, J. P. (1972). *Eleanor: The years alone.* New York, NY: Norton & Company Inc.

London, N. (1991). The concept of the high school in an emerging society: An analysis of major trends. *Canadian and International Education, 20*(2), 54–70.

London, N. (1996). Quality control in a colonial setting: How it worked and for what purpose? *Canadian and International Education, 25*(1), 43–61.

Meighan, R. (1986). *A sociology of educating.* London: Cassell Educational Ltd.

Miller, C. M. L., & Parlett, M. (1983). *Up to the mark.* London: SRHE.

Miller, E. (1996). Literacy, gender and high schooling. In D. Craig (Ed.). *Education in the West Indies: Developments and perspectives (1948–1988)* (pp. 47–74). Kingston: The University of the West Indies.

Moore, B., & Johnson, M. A. (2004). *Neither led nor driven: Contesting British Cultural imperialism (1865–1920).* Mona: University of the West Indies Press.

Pitman, A., & Chishtie, F. A. (2004). Pakistan: The state, religion and school mathematics. *Canadian and International Education, 33*(2), 31–56.

Poonwassie, D. (1991). Political influence and curriculum change: The case of Guyana. *Canadian and International Education, 20*(2), 42–53.

Rodham Clinton, H. (2014). *Hard choices*. New York, NY: Simon and Schuster.

Sheldon, N. (2015). *History examinations from the 1960s to the present day*. Retrieved from https://www.history.ac.UK/.../history-examinations-from-the 1960s-to-the-present-day.doc

Shepard, L. (2000). The role of assessment in a learning culture. *Educational Researcher, 29*(7), 4–14.

Tweed, R. G., & Lehman. D. R. (2002). Learning considered within a cultural context. *American Psychologist, 57*(2), 89–99.

Wang, R. (1995). *The blind men and the elephant*. Retrieved from https://www.cs.princeton.edu/~rywang/berkeley/258/parable.html

World Educational Services (WES). (n.d.). *Moving the agenda along: A WES stakeholder forum on advancing credential recognition*. Retrieved from http://www.wes.org/ca/immigrants/stakeholderforumsnapshot.pdf

Wright, H. K. (1993). What is Shakespeare doing in my hut? 'A' level literature in the Sierra Leonean student. *Canadian and International Education, 22*(1), 66–85.

CHAPTER 3

A Tale of Two Education Systems

Kim Koh

Over the past two decades, education reforms around the world have led to a wide range of initiatives, including curriculum redesign with a focus on cross-curricular competencies (i.e., 21st-century competencies); international comparisons of students' performance on mathematics, science, and reading; teachers' capacity building in the design and use of inquiry-based pedagogical approaches and alternative forms of assessment; and investment in initial teacher preparation and inservice teacher professional development programs. These various initiatives were launched with an eye toward improving the quality of teachers' instructional practices and increasing equitable learning opportunities for students, which in turn contribute to better student learning outcomes.

To provide every student with the opportunity to learn and master competencies across curricula, K–12 teachers are expected to be knowledgeable in the design, selection, and use of a repertoire of assessment methods such as authentic assessment, performance assessment, formative assessment, assessment for learning, diagnostic assessment, dynamic assessment, and stealth assessment (e.g., game-based assessment). These assessment methods are alternatives to traditional standardized paper-and-pen tests and aim to enable students to demonstrate what they know and can do through their performance on richer authentic intellectual tasks (Newmann, Marks, & Gamoran, 1996). In addition, formative assessment or assessment for learning are deemed to promote students' self-directed learning skills and growth mindsets through the provision of timely and quality feedback from the teacher and peers as well as students' active engagement in self-assessment and metacognitive activities (assessment as learning, Earl, 2003). To adopt these student-centered assessment methods effectively, teachers need not only to improve their assessment literacy (e.g., Koh, 2011; Stiggins, 1995), but also to change their beliefs about student learning (Song & Koh, 2010) as well as their conceptions of the true purpose of assessment (Brown, 2011).

According to Hargreaves, Earl, and Schmidt (2002), "The challenge of assessment reform is one of the re-culturing or rethinking the nature and purpose of classroom assessment" (p. 76). Many teachers were exposed to traditional modes of assessments and pedagogies entailing standardized testing and didactic teaching while they were students in K–12 schools and in post-secondary/tertiary education, including preservice teacher education. Yet, global educational reform movements have increasingly called for a shift toward student- or learner-centered pedagogical approaches (e.g., problem-based learning, project-based learning, inquiry-based learning, case-based learning, game-based learning), characterized by constructivist teaching and alternative forms of assessment. The aim is to promote students' learning and mastery of essential 21st-century competencies such as higher-order thinking, complex problem-solving, creativity and innovation, effective communication, collaboration, and self-directed learning. In an era of knowledge-based, globalized economies, these competencies are valued over rote memorization, routine problem-solving or mechanical skills, or the reproduction of knowledge. As stated by Darling-Hammond and Adamson (2010), "High-achieving nations have pointed all of the elements [design curriculum, organize teaching, and assess learning] of their systems toward challenging tasks that require students to use sophisticated knowledge to solve complex problems and explain their reasoning" (p. 1). Taken together, these suggest that developing teachers' assessment literacy and their conceptions of the true purpose of classroom assessment is more important than ever if educators intend to provide equitable learning opportunities for all students, rather than just a privileged few, to learn and master 21st-century competencies (Rotherham & Willingham, 2009).

For this chapter, I purposefully selected two education systems, that of Alberta, Canada and Singapore, to examine how teachers' assessment literacy can be improved through high-quality teacher preparation and professional development programs. Despite their different sociocultural and geopolitical contexts, both educational systems have invested heavily, and striven toward improving the quality of teaching and student learning through curricular reforms and new assessment initiatives. Policymakers in both systems are forward-looking and have made intentional efforts to revamp K–12 curriculum and to improve teachers' instructional and assessment practices, with an ultimate goal of providing every student with an equitable opportunity to learn and master the essential 21st-century competencies.

I begin the chapter by describing the sociocultural and policy contexts of Alberta and Singapore. I then discuss a selection of case studies that demonstrate instances of student performance in international assessments, curriculum redesign, assessment-related policy initiatives, and investment in initial teacher preparation and inservice professional development programs. The discussion is followed by a comparison of how teacher preparation and professional development programs in both educational systems create professional learning opportunities for preservice and inservice teachers to develop their assessment literacy in light of global education reforms. I conclude the chapter with two sets of recommendations for (1) improving the quality of assessment curriculum in initial teacher preparation programs, and (2) enhancing the quality of professional development programs in assessment for both preservice and inservice teachers.

Comparative National Contexts

As aptly pointed out by Hiebert and Stigler (2017), "A significant benefit of cross-cultural studies is the eye-opening awareness that comes from comparing one's own country with practices in other countries" (p. 169). This leads to a comparison of the following sociocultural and policy contexts in Alberta and Singapore.

Alberta, Canada

Alberta is Canada's fourth most-populous province, with an estimated population of 4.33 million as of 2019. It is located within the western region of Canada and has abundant natural resources (predominantly, oil and gas). Its geographic area is about 254,827 square miles. Its thriving economy, proximity to the beautiful Rocky Mountains and rolling grassland prairie, and generally good standard of living have made Alberta one of the popular destinations for internal migration and external international immigration. Calgary, a cosmopolitan city in Alberta, has been consistently ranked as one of the top ten most liveable cities in the world. In 2018, Calgary is ranked the No. 4 most liveable city in the world (The Economist Intelligent Unit, 2018). With the changes in federal immigration policies, there has been a growing number of immigrant students who speak English as a Second language (ESL) or English as a Foreign Language (EFL) in K–12 schools and higher education institutions across Canada's ten provinces and three territories. Both federal and provincial governments are elected democratically by Canadian citizens. Alberta's government is formed by the political party that wins the periodic provincial general election. Thus, a change in provincial government may have implications for educational policies, that is, one government may continue or terminate another government's initiatives. For example, the New Democratic Party (NDP), elected as a new majority, took over the Alberta government from the Progressive Conservative (PC) Party in 2015. The NDP government invested CAD $64 million into an overhaul of the provincial K–12 school curricula (Bennett, 2016). Despite some controversies, the curricula overhaul is planned to be completed in three phases: K–4 by 2018, Grades 5–8 by 2019, and Grades 9–12 by 2022. The new K–4 curriculum is being tested in selected Alberta schools in the winter of 2019. However, the NDP lost the provincial election in the spring of 2019. The newly elected government, led by the United Conservative Party (UCP), has pledged to scrap the NDP's curriculum overhaul.

Since 2015, the province has moved toward the design, pilot testing, and implementation of Student Learning Assessments (SLAs, Theobald, 2015). In fact, SLAs were a key policy initiative by the old PC government designed as an alternative to the Provincial Achievement Tests in Grades 3, 6, and 9. The original intent of SLAs was to serve as diagnostic assessments to provide informative feedback to students and parents and to promote teachers' use of assessment data to inform their instructional plans and improve students' learning in core subject areas. After pilot testing the Grade 3 SLA in the 2016–17 school year, teachers raised concerns about the amount of work involved in administering and scoring SLAs and the timing of both administration of SLAs and the release of assessment results to the key stakeholders. Due to these concerns, the NDP government announced in 2017 that starting in the 2017–18 school year, Grade 3 teachers could use their professional judgment to determine whether to administer SLA to their students. In the spring of 2019, the fate is SLAs is unknown as the UCP government has determined to reintroduce back-to-basics pedagogical approaches and high-stakes testing in the early grades.

Singapore
As a nation-state, Singapore appears as a little red dot on a world map, located at the southern tip of peninsular Malaysia. It is one of the smallest countries in Southeast Asia but has the highest GDP (Gross domestic product). The country is only 276.5 square miles, almost ten times smaller than Alberta. It is a man-made garden city and is one of the fastest-growing metropolitan cities in the world. Its population is 5.84 million as of 2019. There are three main ethnic groups: Chinese, Malay, and Indian. Although English is the official language in governmental agencies and serves as the medium of instruction in Singapore's schools, students from each of the ethnic groups are expected to learn their respective mother tongue at school (e.g., ethnic Chinese students learn Mandarin, while ethnic Malay students learn the Malay language). A lack of natural resources has led the government of Singapore to heavily invest in building human capital through high-quality education ranging from K–12 schools to higher education institutions. This suggests the importance of having a strong teaching workforce; hence, the quality of teachers and teacher education is of paramount importance.

After achieving independence from Malaysia in 1965, Singapore transformed from being a fishing village to becoming a world economic and education powerhouse. Singaporean teachers and educators have played pivotal roles in educating Singaporean children and youth over three broad phases of education: survival-driven phase (1959 to 1978), efficiency-driven phase (1979 to 1996), and ability-based, aspiration-driven phase (1997 to the present day). See Goh and Gopinathan (2008) for a detailed description of each of the phases. At the turn of the 21st century, Singapore became a global sensation for her students' continuing success in international assessments such as the Trends in International Mathematics and Science Study (TIMSS), the Progress in International Reading Literacy Study (PIRLS), and the Program for International Student Assessment (PISA). Despite its international stature, the Singapore Ministry of Education (MOE) has continued learning and adopting the best practices from other developed countries (Goodwin, 2012). A meritocratic system has driven the efficient execution of high-stakes national examinations in Grades 6, 9, and 12. Many Singaporean teachers and parents are proud of their students' or children's stellar performance in the Primary School Leaving Exam (PSLE, Grade 6), the Cambridge O-level exam (Grade 9), and the Cambridge A-level exam (Grade 12). The summative scores derived from these exams are used to determine students' future academic and career pathways.

To ensure that students receive the best education, preservice teachers who undertake their one-year Postgraduate Diploma in Education (PGDE) are carefully selected from the top 30% of applicants. Like Finland, teaching is one of the highly regarded professions in Singapore; MOE ensures that teachers are paid handsomely, have the best working conditions, and are provided lifelong professional learning opportunities. For example, every Singaporean teacher is entitled to 100 hours of release time ("white space") per year to participate in professional development workshops or graduate courses. The Academy of Singapore Teachers is established by MOE to provide teachers with professional learning opportunities such as conferences, forums, and seminars. Those seeking M.A. and Ph.D. degrees at the National Institute of Education Singapore (NIE) or abroad can apply for study leave. In addition, many are offered graduate scholarships from either the MOE or the NIE. Taken together, these suggest that the Singaporean government has used various incentives to attract, develop, and retain the best teachers. In a study commissioned by the McKinsey and Company, Singapore has been identified as one of the top-performing education systems in the world that benefits from a high-quality teacher workforce (Auguste, Kihn, & Miller, 2010).

Since the launch of the "Thinking Schools Learning Nation" initiative in 1997 by Gok Chong Tong, then Prime Minister of Singapore, three new assessment initiatives were carefully implemented by the MOE to create a wider opportunity for students to move beyond "drill-and-practice" examination strategies.

They were Science Practical Assessment (SPA), project work, and Strategies for Active and Independent Learning (SAIL). SPA was designed as a school-based performance assessment. It assesses students' science practical skills over a period of time and counts toward 20% of the overall marks for the subject in Singapore-Cambridge GCE Ordinary Level examination. Project work was introduced to both elementary and secondary schools to assess students' 21st-century competencies. As a self-assessment strategy, SAIL provides students the opportunity to assess and monitor their own learning. Despite these innovative assessment approaches, high-stakes national examinations (i.e., PSLE, O- and A-level exams) administering to students in Grades 6, 9, and 12 remain the key determinants of Singaporean students' successes in their future studies and careers. At the point of writing, the author read that the Singapore government has announced major changes to the assessments for some grade levels starting in 2019. These changes will be discussed later in this chapter.

Student Performance in International Assessments

Students in both the Alberta and Singapore education systems have demonstrated stellar performance in international assessments, such as the PISA and the TIMSS. PISA is developed by the Organization for Economic Cooperation and Development (OECD) to measure 15-year-old students' mathematics, science, and reading literacy. It is conducted in countries around the world every three years. The word "literacy" connotes the ability to apply knowledge and skills to solve real-world problems. For example, mathematical literacy refers to the ability to estimate or make conjectures; interpret data; solve complex problems; communicate using mathematics; and reason in numerical, graphical, and geometric situations. TIMSS is developed by the International Association for the Evaluation of Educational Achievement (IEA) to measure Grades 4 and 8 students' achievement in mathematics and science. It is administered in countries or education systems around the world every four years. Data derived from the PISA and TIMSS are used for cross-national comparisons of students' performance. Such comparisons serve high-stakes accountability purposes, as they are used by policymakers and the media to make inferences about the quality of education in participating countries.

Compared to TIMSS, the focus of PISA is on "how well students are prepared to meet the challenges of the future, rather than how well they master particular curricula" (OECD, 2012, p. 3). In terms of the nature of assessment, the items in TIMSS are more knowledge-oriented and are designed to measure students' achievement of textbook-like knowledge and skills. In contrast, PISA includes more performance-based tasks that aim to capture students' demonstration of what they know and can do in authentic contexts. In other words, TIMSS is about students' mastery of knowledge while PISA is about students' demonstration of understanding through their application of knowledge to solve real-world problems (i.e., literacy). Since its inception in 2000, a specific subject is selected as the major focus in each cycle of PISA. The subject that became a major focus in PISA was measured and reported on its overall student performance and scores on specific content areas. The other two subjects serving as minor domains were only measured and reported for their overall scores. For example, mathematical literacy was the major focus in PISA 2003 and 2012 while scientific literacy was reported in PISA 2006 and 2015.

Singapore's students were among the top in the world in mathematics and science on both TIMSS and PISA. In 2015, Singapore's students ranked first, in science (major focus), reading, and mathematics (minor domains) in PISA, which was administered to 15-year-old students in 72 countries. In contrast, although Alberta's students were among the highest achievers in the world in mathematics, science, and reading, their performance in mathematics significantly declined from 2003 to 2012. A similar trend was observed in other Canadian provinces. As reported by the Council of Ministers of Education, Canada (CMEC, 2012), "Canadian students performed consistently well in mathematics over the last nine years, but there is a clear trend showing a decrease in average score in most provinces, as well as an increase in the number of countries outperforming Canada" (p. 31). In PISA 2015, Canada's students, including those from Alberta, demonstrated excellent scientific literacy. According to the CMEC (2015) report, Canadian students' performance did not change between 2006 and 2015. On TIMSS, Alberta Grade 4 students were found to perform worse on mathematics over the years as, there was a 40-point drop from 1995 to 2015. In addition, Alberta students performed significantly below the mean Canadian score in the 2015 mathematics assessment.

Given the nature of the performance tasks in PISA, the PISA data can provide insight into how effectively countries are preparing students to use mathematics and science in solving real-word problems. Students' mathematical and scientific literacy is a prerequisite for their pursuits of science, technology, engineering, and mathematics (STEM) majors and career pathways. In TIMSS and PISA, students in the US have consistently performed worse than students in other developed countries. The Soviet Union's successful launch of Sputnik in 1957 took the world, including the US, by surprise. As a result, the US government determined to be the world's superpower in science, technology, and engineering. The mediocre performance of US students in TIMSS and PISA has triggered a fresh wave of concerns. Moreover, a survey conducted by the US

Department of Education in 2010 showed that only 16 percent of high school students were interested in a STEM career and had adequate mathematical proficiency. These alarming statistics led to President Obama's announcement that he would make the improvement of STEM education one of his administration's top priorities (Robelen, 2011). Since then, STEM has become a global policy initiative. In many countries including Canada, there has been a clarion call to build a strong STEM workforce through innovative STEM curricula, instruction, and assessment in K-12 schools (National Academy of Engineering and National Research Council, 2014). This, in turn, will contribute to a nation's innovation capacity, economic prosperity, and social well-being in an increasingly complex and competitive globalized world.

Redesigning Curriculum for 21st-Century Competencies

Both Alberta and Singapore have placed great emphasis on the continuing review and redesign of K–12 curricula in light of global educational reforms. The launch of the Framework for 21st Century Learning by the Partnership for 21st Century Skills (2002) drives curricular reforms and assessment innovations in many education systems around the world. According to the Framework for 21st Century Learning, students need to move beyond mastery of core subject knowledge. Public school systems are urged to take the responsibility to prepare students for a knowledge-based global economy that values critical thinking, complex problem-solving, innovation and creativity, effective communication, good collaboration, self-directed and lifelong learning, and active and responsible citizenship, to name a few. The Partnership for 21st Century Skills (2002) works to encourage K–12 schools and higher education institutions to incorporate these essential 21st-century competencies into the teaching of core subjects.

A survey conducted by the Partnership for 21st Century Skills (2008) found that the top five competencies or skills employers sought in potential employees in the US were professionalism, teamwork/collaboration, oral communication, ethics and social responsibility, and reading comprehension. Hodge and Lear (2011) analyzed and compared the top five competencies/skills sought by employers based on the surveys conducted by the Partnership for 21st Century Skills, the National Association of Colleges and Employers, and the American Management Association. The authors found that communication and collaboration were two competencies commonly identified across the three surveys. Other competencies included critical thinking and problem-solving, creativity and innovation, technical literacy, and strong work ethic.

To ensure that every student has an equitable opportunity for learning and mastering the 21st-century competencies, the governments in Alberta and Singapore revamped school curricula. In 2009, the MOE Singapore developed and launched its framework for 21st-century competencies and desired student outcomes. The desired educational outcomes for Singaporean students are to become a confident person, a self-directed learner, a concerned citizen, and an active contributor to society. To enable students to achieve these outcomes, the following 21st-century competencies are incorporated into school curricula: critical and inventive thinking, civic literacy, global awareness, cross-cultural skills, and information and communication skills. This set of desired student outcomes is also referred to as soft or non-academic skills.

In Alberta, the Framework for Student Learning (Alberta Education, 2011) serves as a signpost for designing and implementing curriculum and assessment in K–12 schools. It includes the following competencies as the desired educational outcomes: critical thinking, problem solving and decision making; creativity and innovation; communication; collaboration and leadership; digital and technological literacy; social, cultural, global and environmental responsibility; and lifelong learning, personal management and well-being.

Students' learning and mastery of these competencies cut across all subject areas, ranging from language arts to mathematics to sciences and technology. The ultimate goal is to enable Alberta students to become engaged thinkers and ethical citizens who also possess an entrepreneurial spirit. The desired students' outcomes were fully elaborated in Alberta Education's (2010) Inspiring Education policy document. With the change of provincial government in 2015, a new framework was introduced, that is, the Guiding Framework for the Design and Development of Kindergarten to Grade 12 Provincial Curriculum—Programs of Study. It outlines a set of essential learning outcomes including subject-specific conceptual and procedural knowledge, cross-curricular competencies, and core values for all Alberta students to achieve. The values include "democracy and citizenship, belonging and identity, integrity and respect, perseverance and excellence, and innovation and stewardship" (Alberta Education, 2016, p. 3). The framework also includes the Alberta government's policy initiatives and commitments to "economic diversification, climate change, wellness, pluralism, diversity, inclusion, First Nations, Métis and Inuit education for reconciliation, rights of Indigenous peoples, and Francophone cultures and perspectives" (Alberta Education, 2016, p. 1). Taken together, these provincial education outcomes represent those desired by the Federal Government.

In short, both curriculum frameworks in Singapore and Alberta focus on students' mastery of skills and competencies that prepare them to succeed in the 21st-century workplace and society. This means students need to go beyond acquisition of content knowledge in core subject areas. Hence, teachers are urged to infuse the 21st-century competencies into core academic subjects by using innovative pedagogical approaches and alternative forms of assessment that are focused on the learners. From a social-constructivist learning paradigm, student-centered assessments value the use of authentic and formative assessments to support students' learning (Shepard, 2000). The paradigm contrasts significantly with the behaviorist learning theory that espouses objectivity and uniformity of standardized testing.

Assessment, Teaching, and Learning

Under the influences of behaviorist learning theory, instruction and assessment are treated as two separate entities (Shepard, 2000). Generally, the mindsets or beliefs of many teachers, parents, and policymakers are shaped by behaviorist learning theory and the standardized testing paradigm due to their past educational experiences. As such, classroom practices of most teachers tend to be dominated by summative assessments that epitomize objective measurement of discrete facts and procedures. Consequently, students are passively involved in rote recall and reproduction of knowledge as a given. The adverse effects of summative assessments on teaching and learning are well known. Assessment is merely conducted at the end of teaching and learning (i.e., assessment of learning) to measure how much a student has learned as compared to his peers (i.e., norm-referenced). To increase students' test/exam scores, teachers' assessment practices in the day-to-day classroom may mimic the content and form of high-stakes accountability tests or national exams (i.e., teaching to the tests/exams). Teachers' job performance is often appraised by school administrators based on students' achievement. A heavy focus on using students' test scores to reward or sanction teachers can be detrimental to teachers' instructional practices and students' learning. For examples, see Chapter 2 of this book.

Compared to the behaviorist learning theory and standardized testing paradigm, social-constructivist learning theory deems that assessment is an integral part of instruction. As pointed out by Shepard (2000), assessment should be used to promote a learning culture in the day-to-day classrooms. Assessment needs to serve learning purposes (i.e., assessment for and as learning) rather than testing simply for accountability purposes (i.e., assessment of learning). Assessment for learning practices include explicit sharing of success criteria with learners, formative feedback, effective questioning, self- and peer assessment, and dynamic assessment. Under the social-constructivist learning theory, students' development of cognitive abilities is mediated by social interactions and support/scaffolding from experts and peers (i.e., Vygotsky's zone of proximal development). Hence, assessment and learning are primarily social processes. According to Lorrie Shepard (2000), former President of the American Educational Research Association:

> Classroom routines and the ways that teachers and students talk with each other should help students gain experience with the ways of thinking and speaking in academic disciplines. School learning should be authentic and connected to the world outside of school not only to make learning more interesting and motivating to students but also to develop the ability to use knowledge in real-world settings. (p. 7)

Shepard (2000) also pointed out the importance of fostering students' dispositions or soft skills, which include persistence in solving complex problems. Although Shepard (2000) did not use the term "authentic assessment," she raised two essential aspects of realigning classroom assessment to the social-constructivist model of teaching and learning. First, realignment requires the form and content of classroom assessment to better capture higher-order learning outcomes such as critical thinking and problem-solving skills in academic disciplines. Second, teachers and students must change their mindsets about the purposes and functions of assessment. To create an equitable, supportive, and inclusive learning environment for every student, teachers' and students' conceptions need to undergo a profound shift from using classroom assessment for accountability (assessment of learning or summative assessment) to learning purposes (assessment for learning or formative assessment) (Brown, 2011; Stiggins, 2002).

Shepard's (2000) first recommendation for changing forms of assessment follows Wiggins's (1989) and Newmann et al.'s (1996) notions of authentic assessment. Wiggins (1989) defined authentic assessment as assessment tasks that replicate real-world challenges and standards of performance that experts or professionals typically face in the discipline or field. Authentic assessments are more effective than traditional standardized tests in measuring students' intellectual achievement or cognitive ability. This is because authentic assessments enable students to demonstrate their deep understanding, higher-order thinking, and complex problem-solving through performing real-world tasks (Koh, 2017). Newmann, Bryk, and Nagaoka (2001) have indicated that one important criterion for students to engage in authentic intellectual work is disciplined inquiry, which means that students are actively engaged in making elaborated written and/or oral communication regarding their understanding, reasoning, arguments, explanations, and conclusions. In addition, their ability to construct or produce new knowledge is supported by disciplined inquiry.

Shepard's (2000) second realignment suggests that teachers need to place greater emphasis on formative assessment or assessment for learning. This means assessment should support teaching and learning in the day-to-day classroom. This follows Black and Wiliam's (1998a) seminal work on a meta-analysis of the effect of formative assessment on students' achievement and their classic article titled "Assessment and Classroom Learning" (Black & Wiliam, 1998b). They found that formative assessment yielded significant gains on students' achievement. Shepard also advocates the use of authentic assessment and formative assessment for learning that make learning more interesting and motivating to students and develop students' 21st-century competencies, and these sorts of assessments are highly valued in contemporary K–12 classrooms.

Investment in Teacher Preparation and Professional Development

Both the Singapore and Alberta education systems have invested money and resources in improving the quality of intial teacher preparation and inservice professional development programs. In Alberta, the Alberta Initiative for School Improvement (AISI) program was a bold strategy for province-wide school improvement (Parsons & Hewson, 2014). The program supported a wide range of projects that aimed to improve the quality of student learning across different school jurisdictions. Key stakeholders, including teachers, school administrators, trustees, parents, and the community, were encouraged to work together to introduce innovative and creative initiatives. To improve the quality of student learning, principals acted as instructional leaders, creating a supportive and collegial environment to support teachers' innovative pedagogical and assessment practices. AISI was an exemplary model of how the government partnered with school administrators (i.e., superintendents and principals), teachers, teacher educators, educational researchers, and local communities to support school improvement initiatives (Hargreaves et al., 2009). School improvement is a collective enterprise which can only be achieved by sustainable research partnership and effective instructional leadership rather than the "aggressive supervision and evaluation of teachers" (Parsons & Hewson, 2014, p. 7). Schools and school boards were given the autonomy and flexibility to propose a range of improvement strategies in their AISI research. The strategies were related to three province-wide themes: professional learning communities, differentiated instruction, and assessment for learning. These themes became the AISI priority areas because they reflected the global trends at the turn of the 21st century.

Between the fiscal years 2000 to 2012, the Alberta Government allocated more than CAD500 million to the AISI program (AISI Education Partners, 2008). Numerous schools seized upon the funding opportunities to embark on action research in many areas, especially in assessment for learning. Snapshots of evidence showed a positive impact of AISI on school improvement. However, conclusions on the effects on student learning outcomes cannot be drawn due to a lack of student-level data (Crocker, 2009). After three successful cycles of AISI, the Alberta government reduced 50% of its budget to support AISI grants in the fourth cycle. In 2013, the funding was terminated due to budget constraints in Alberta. However, the government continues to encourage the implementation of AISI findings and best practices with the vision for "Inspiring Education" (Alberta Education, 2010). The "Inspiring Education" has been replaced with the "Guiding Framework for the Design and Development of Kindergarten to Grade 12 Provincial Curriculum—Programs of Study (Alberta Education, 2016), and a province-wide curriculum redesign was introduced by the Alberta government. From 2017 to 2019, Alberta Education supported three cycles of Research Partner School Initiative through conditional grants awarded to university researchers and school teachers who collaborate in research projects that address important research priority areas identified by the government.

The 2007 McKinsey study rated Singapore as one of the best-performing education systems in the world (Barber & Mourshed, 2007). Since the launch of the "Thinking Schools, Learning Nation" (TSLN) vision in 1997 by Goh Chok Tong, then Prime Minister of Singapore, MOE implemented various curriculum and assessment initiatives across different schooling levels with an eye toward students' development of 21st-century competencies. Specifically, TSLN aims to build "a nation of thinking and committed citizens capable of meeting the challenges of the future, and an education system geared to the needs of the 21st century" (MOE, 2010, p. 3). A Learning Nation envisions a national culture or social environment that promotes lifelong learning in her citizens. At the time, the TSLN vision led to two major initiatives, namely curriculum reviews in all core subject areas and introducing authentic assessments (e.g., project work, SPA) and formative assessment (e.g., SAIL) in Singaporean schools. Authentic assessments enrich students' learning experiences because the tasks provide students with the opportunity to synthesize knowledge from various areas of learning. Students are also required to: critically and creatively apply knowledge and skills to solve complex problems in real-world contexts; actively engage in making extended communication; effectively collaborating with their peers in accomplishing a common goal or completing a task; and be resourceful and independent in learning (e.g., searching for information or reference materials in the library and over the Internet). Project work,

SPA, and SAIL were designed by the Singapore Examinations and Assessment Board (SEAB), a government-owned testing agency which is responsible for the development and administration of national exams in Singapore. Teachers were involved in the implementation of project work, SPA, and SAIL as school-based assessments. Although the original purposes of SPA and project work were to promote inquiry-based, authentic learning experiences in students, some teachers had implemented the assessments in a traditional way. This is because students' performance in SPA and project work counted towards the final grades in GCE 'O' Level exam and the admission criteria to local universities, respectively (Koh, 2014a).

To ensure that Singapore schools are preparing students for the global knowledge economy, the Singapore government recognizes the importance of shifting the education system toward a focus on innovation and evidence-based practice in classroom pedagogy and assessment. As such, a research center was established in 2002 at the National Institute of Education (NIE) at the Nanyang Technological University. NIE is the sole teacher training college in Singapore. The research center was named the Centre for Research in Pedagogy and Practice (CRPP), and the founding Dean was Professor Allan Luke, a world-renowned teacher educator, researcher, university administrator, and ministerial advisor. MOE invested $36 million into the first CORE Research Program (2003–2006) that enabled a research team led by Professor Allan Luke to conduct a large-scale evidence-based study to inform government policies in relation to curriculum, pedagogy, and assessment. The CORE program was one of the world's largest government-funded research studies that employed multi-level, multiple methodologies to provide a rigorous empirical description of classroom pedagogy and assessment (Luke, 2011). More important, the CORE research findings led to evidence-based policy making in Singapore.

In 2004, Prime Minister Lee Hsien Loong announced the vision of "Teach Less, Learn More" (TLLM) at the National Day Rally. TLLM was officially launched as a policy in 2005 by the then Minister of Education, Tharman Shamugaratnam. As a continuation of TSLN, TLLM calls for teachers to emphasize the depth rather than the breadth of teaching and learning. Despite the introduction of TSLN for nearly a decade, most Singaporean classrooms were characterized by "traditional chalk-and-talk," rote learning, and conventional assessments (i.e., worksheets, summative tests). This was evidenced by Luke and his co-authors' empirical findings derived from a large representative sample of Singaporean schools. In his distinguished lecture at the 2011 American Educational Research Association (AERA) annual meeting, Luke (2011) aptly summed up these features in Singaporean classrooms, "high levels of time-on-task, teacher-center pedagogy that is focused on curriculum content, and a very strong emphasis on basic skills" (Luke, 2011, p. 374). In addition, teachers' assessment practices tended to focus on summative assessment of learning and conventional assessment tasks that reinforce students' regurgitation and reproduction of facts and procedures (Koh & Luke, 2009).

As a result of the CORE research findings, the TLLM policy initiative called for teachers to shift their pedagogical and assessment practices toward more learner-centered instruction and a better focus on the holistic development of students' academic and non-academic skills. There is also a clarion call for Singaporean teachers to utilize alternative forms of assessment that yield multiple sources of evidence of students' learning rather than using a single score based on traditional standardized tests or high-stakes national exams. An excerpt from the then Minister of Education Tharman Shamugaratnam (2005) is included below:

> We have to shift from our heavily examination-oriented system if we are to achieve the goals in education that I described earlier and develop the critical life skills that our young need for the future. We must arouse a passion among our young for knowledge and learning that carries through life. We have to place equal emphasis on the non-academic curriculum that will help them make the most of their years together in school interacting, roughing it out with each other and making friendships. And most fundamentally, we have to accept and promote more diverse measures of merit, even if they cannot be summarized in a single score.

As Tan (2008) aptly points out, the Singapore government is forward looking in introducing education reforms; however, the implementation of reforms has been done in a tactical manner. To promote students' mastery of academic and non-academic skills at the elementary level, the Primary Education Review and Implementation Committee of MOE tried out "bite-sized assessments" (i.e., formative assessments) in Grades 1 and 2 in 2010 (MOE, 2009a). With fewer high-stakes exams (i.e., summative assessments) during these formative years, students are given more time and space to develop non-cognitive skills or dispositions such as confidence and desire to learn, self-directed learning, active participation, and responsible citizenship (MOE, 2009a). During the same year, the Secondary Education Review and Implementation Committee (MOE, 2010) recommended secondary school curricula and assessments to place greater emphasis on "the inculcation of learning and life skills, values, character and citizenship, socio-emotional competencies among secondary school students" (Tan, Koh, & Choy, pp. 136–137).

After a few successful trials of PERI and SERI recommendations, MOE finally announced several changes to the school examination system (Ong, 2018). Starting in 2019, weighted assessments and examinations for grades 1 and 2 students will be removed. Additionally, mid-term examinations (summative assessments) will be eliminated for grade 7 students in 2019 and for grades 3, 5, and 9 students in 2020 and 2021. Such changes will significantly reduce the assessment load of both teachers and students. In the 2018 Schools Work Plan Seminar, Minister of Education Ong Ye Kung urged Singaporean teachers to "pace out teaching and learning" and to "leverage effective inquiry-based pedagogies to enhance students' learning experiences" (Ong, 2018, pp. 5–6). By reducing summative assessments, Singaporean students are being given more time and space to enjoy the learning process, as well as to deepen their conceptual understanding and develop 21st-century competencies.[1] After all, the ultimate goal of education is to enable students to become independent and lifelong learners who possess the grit and resilience to overcome challenges in an ever changing and unpredictable world.

Compared to teachers in other developed countries, Singaporean teachers were supported by having more time and space to develop their capabilities through inservice teacher education and professional development programs. For example, MOE provided up to $100,000 as additional funds for elementary schools that demonstrated strong school-based professional development programs. Such financial support enables school administrators to create "white space" for teachers to engage in school-based professional learning communities and action research. Compared to other high-performing education systems including Alberta, the Singaporean government has consistently provided both scholarships and resources to support Singaporean teachers to take part in continuous professional learning and development (Goodwin, Low, & Darling-Hammond, 2017; Low, Goodwin, & Snyder, 2017). Using the Finnish model of teacher education (Sahlberg, 2011) as an exemplar, MOE encourages inservice teachers in Singapore to upgrade their educational qualifications at NIE and abroad. From 2005 to 2009, NIE developed and offered new graduate programs to teachers who responded to the call of MOE. The programs included a M.Ed. in Curriculum and Teaching and a Masters in Teaching. Additionally, in partnership with Teachers College, Columbia University, the NIE launched the first Master of Arts in Leadership and Educational Change in 2012. From 2007 to 2017, NIE worked with the Institute of Education, University College London to offer Doctor of Education (Ed.D.) (Dual Award) program to promote the quality of teachers and school administrators (e.g., principals, vice principals). In 2012, NIE's own Ed.D. program was launched for the first time, with the vision to build the professional capacity of teachers, departmental or subject heads, and school administrators that are uniquely Singapore. These initiatives have resulted in an exponential increase in the number of teachers, departmental or subject heads, and school administrators who earn at least a master's degree.

Developing Teachers' Assessment Literacy

Since the launch of the Framework for 21st Century Learning by the Partnership for 21st Century Skills (2002), initial teacher preparation and graduate programs for inservice teachers in many higher education institutions around the globe have focused on the development of assessment literacy in both preservice and inservice teachers. Teachers' assessment literacy or competence is one of the key professional standards for teacher certification, licensure, and evaluation in many education systems around the world. Assessment-literate teachers are capable of: using a repertoire of assessment methods based on sound assessment principles, aligning classroom assessments with the intended learner outcomes in the curriculum; designing, selecting, and using high-quality assessment tasks that accurately capture students' learning and performance in core subjects and students' demonstration of cross-curricular competencies; striking a balance between formative assessment (assessment for and as learning) and summative assessment (assessment of learning); understanding the purposes of classroom and large-scale assessments; interpreting and using assessment data to inform instructional practice and student learning. In Alberta, for example, preservice and inservice teachers' assessment literacy is represented by indicators of effective assessment practices to optimize the learning of every student and the assessment indicators are subsumed under "professional body of knowledge" in the Teaching Quality Standard (Alberta Government, 2018). In Singapore, preservice and inservice teachers' assessment literacy is defined by their professional knowledge of the following elements: diagnoses of student needs and learning process; assessment principles, forms, and procedures (e.g., purposes and functions of formative and summative assessments); analysis and use of student data to adjust instructional practice and to support student learning; and research (e.g., awareness of research on teaching and resources for professional learning, use of research to inform practice and decision making). Teachers' assessment literacy is one of the key professional standards in MOE's teaching competency model (NIE, 2009).

Table 3.1 presents a summary of the assessment courses offered at both preservice and inservice teacher education levels in higher education institutions in Alberta and Singapore.

TABLE 3.1   Assessment courses in Alberta's and Singapore's Higher Education Institutions (adapted from Koh, Lock, Paris, & Niayesh, 2016)

Countries/ Institutions	Course/Program/ Year	Objectives	Learning outcomes
Alberta, Canada University of Calgary	*Assessment* in B.Ed. Program Year 2 Term 4 (2013–2016) *Assessment* in B.Ed. Program Year 1 Term 2 (starting in 2017)	To enable preservice teachers to develop a deep understanding of the definitions, purposes, functions, and principles of different forms of assessment	– Through the investigation of assessment problems, preservice teachers work through key concepts of measurement, testing, balanced assessment, assessment *of* learning, assessment *for* learning, assessment *as* learning, authentic assessment; review and critique of performance assessment and rubrics; and engage in intellectual discourse on sound grading and reporting practices
	Leading Assessment in M.Ed. Specialist Leading for Learning	To provide an opportunity for inservice teachers, learning leaders, and school administrators to engage in intellectual and scholarly pursuit of the theoretical foundations and current applied developments in the field of student assessment from a leadership perspective considering local, national and international contexts	– To develop an understanding of the role of school leaders in student assessment – To develop an awareness of contemporary issues in student assessment – To develop and extend a knowledge base in student assessment – To develop a critical stance concerning educational assessment theory and practice – To explore and analyze the theoretical foundations of student assessment and the relevance to current assessment practice in Alberta schools

(cont.)

TABLE 3.1   Assessment courses in Alberta's and Singapore's Higher Education Institutions (adapted from Koh, Lock, Paris, & Niayesh, 2016) (cont.)

Countries/ Institutions	Course/Program/ Year	Objectives	Learning outcomes
	Classroom-based Assessment in M.Ed. Interdisciplinary: Leading Assessment	To enhance teachers' and school administrators' understanding of sound classroom assessment practices To engage teachers and school administrators in critical evaluation of the quality of school-based professional development programs in classroom assessment To build teachers' and school administrators' capacity in the design and development of effective professional development programs in classroom assessment	– To develop an understanding of the purposes of classroom assessment and sound classroom assessment practices – To develop an understanding of the design principles and features of authentic assessment, performance assessment, and high-quality rubrics – To develop an understanding of the use of classroom assessment to improve student learning – To develop a critical stance concerning the quality of professional development programs in classroom assessment – To evaluate and redesign professional development programs for building teachers' capacity in classroom assessment

(*cont.*)

TABLE 3.1 Assessment courses in Alberta's and Singapore's Higher Education Institutions (adapted from Koh, Lock, Paris, & Niayesh, 2016) (cont.)

Countries/ Institutions	Course/Program/ Year	Objectives	Learning outcomes
	Assessment and Learning in M.Ed. Interdisciplinary: Assessment and Measurement in Education	To enhance teachers', practitioners', and researchers' understanding of the principles of sound assessment practice, as well as the impact of assessment practices on students' learning in K–12 and post-secondary education settings	– To develop a deeper understanding of the purposes and functions of formative assessment or assessment for learning – To develop an understanding of innovative assessment methods (e.g., stealth assessment, game-based assessment) in supporting student learning – To develop a critical stance toward the role of assessment in creating a supportive learning culture – To empower teachers/instructors to be reflective practitioners in assessment and learning – To build teachers'/instructors' capacity in the design of high-quality assessment tasks and rubrics to promote students' learning and mastery of 21st-century skills and competencies

(*cont.*)

TABLE 3.1 Assessment courses in Alberta's and Singapore's Higher Education Institutions (adapted from Koh, Lock, Paris, & Niayesh, 2016) (*cont.*)

Countries/ Institutions	Course/Program/ Year	Objectives	Learning outcomes
	Basic Statistics for Testing and Measurement in M.Ed. Interdisciplinary: Assessment and Measurement in Education	To develop an understanding of the theoretical frameworks of reliability and validity in terms of educational assessment To conduct statistical analyses using real and simulated student assessment data to develop conclusions for improving school programs and student learning To build teachers' capacity in terms of using student assessment data as a source of information for decision-making to improve teaching and learning	– To utilize statistical methods for comparing group differences – To conduct correlational and categorical analyses – To analyze assessment data to inform decision-making – To use student data for school improvement and effectiveness, as well as improvement in student learning

(*cont.*)

TABLE 3.1 Assessment courses in Alberta's and Singapore's Higher Education Institutions (adapted from Koh, Lock, Paris, & Niayesh, 2016) (cont.)

Countries/ Institutions	Course/Program/ Year	Objectives	Learning outcomes
	Introduction to Test Construction and Measurement in M.Ed. Interdisciplinary: Assessment and Measurement in Education	To enhance teachers' understanding of the basic principles of designing high-quality and effective tests and surveys/ questionnaires	– To develop an understanding of the basic principles of measurement in test/survey construction – To develop an understanding of the steps or procedures in designing high-quality and effective tests and surveys – To develop a critical stance toward the role of tests and surveys in school-based research and in other professional settings – To build capacity in the design, selection, or adaptation of high-quality tests and/surveys for collecting reliable and valid data for use in policy making, program evaluation, instructional planning, and review, and improving student learning and achievement
	Assessment in Technology-Rich Learning Environments M.Ed. Interdisciplinary: Assessment and Measurement in Education	To develop an understanding of the role of technology in assessment within 21st-century learning environments	– To understand the theoretical underpinnings of assessment and learning in technology-rich learning environments – To apply design principles of e-assessment in the context of teaching and learning – To use e-assessments to capture students' mastery of competencies and to support student learning

(cont.)

TABLE 3.1 Assessment courses in Alberta's and Singapore's Higher Education Institutions (adapted from Koh, Lock, Paris, & Niayesh, 2016) (cont.)

Countries/ Institutions	Course/Program/ Year	Objectives	Learning outcomes
	Designed-based Assessment in M.Ed. Specialist: Design-based Learning	To enable teachers to formulate and format assessments in ways that simultaneously afford insights into learners' interpretations and provide learners with cues to extend their own learning	– To reflect on one's conceptions of assessment and learning – To gain a deeper understanding of the relationship between assessment and learning – To develop an understanding of the design principles and features of large-scale assessment, authentic assessment, performance assessment, formative assessment, dynamic assessment, stealth assessment, and rubrics – To learn how to formulate and use assessments to design authentic learning environments that foster learners' disciplinary inquiry and 21st-century competencies (e.g, creative thinking, complex problem-solving, collaboration, communication, self-regulated learning) – To develop an understanding of quality feedback and of how to structure effective feedback loops into a learning environment

(*cont.*)

TABLE 3.1 Assessment courses in Alberta's and Singapore's Higher Education Institutions (adapted from Koh, Lock, Paris, & Niayesh, 2016) (cont.)

Countries/ Institutions	Course/Program/ Year	Objectives	Learning outcomes
	Assessment Practices in Computer-Supported Collaborative Learning in M.Ed. Interdisciplinary: Computer-supported Collaborative Learning (CSCL)	To develop an understanding of the theoretical framework of formative assessment and practical skills in using formative assessment to facilitate CSCL	– To understand the theoretical underpinnings of formative assessment – To understand the opportunities and challenges in using alternative forms of assessment, specifically formative assessment – To plan and use formative assessment in supporting CSCL in authentic settings – To design effective rubrics for assessing collaborative knowledge construction in CSCL environments – To learn how to collaboratively assess student work through professional judgment and effective moderation practices in CSCL environments
University of Alberta	*Educational Assessment* in Year 4 B.Ed. Program	To introduce the complexity of classroom assessment to support and measure student learning	– To develop an understanding of the purposes of assessment and to learn how to match assessment tools to learning objectives, and to analyze the results of both classroom and large-scale assessments to support student learning

(cont.)

TABLE 3.1 Assessment courses in Alberta's and Singapore's Higher Education Institutions (adapted from Koh, Lock, Paris, & Niayesh, 2016) (*cont.*)

Countries/Institutions	Course/Program/Year	Objectives	Learning outcomes
University of Lethbridge	*Curriculum and Assessment for the 21st Century Learner* in M.Ed. Curriculum and Assessment		– To increase knowledge of students' lives to inform 21st-century thinking about curriculum, instruction, and assessment – To articulate developing views about 21st-century learning and technology in the classroom and rethinking curriculum and assessment – To apply students' perceptions to decisions about teaching, learning, and assessment in individual contexts
Singapore: National Institute of Education (NIE), Nanyang Technological University	*Assessing Learning and Performance* in Year 2 Postgraduate Diploma in Education	To provide preservice teachers the ability to understand and apply the basic principles of educational assessment	– To gain the knowledge and skills to monitor, appraise, and evaluate learners' content knowledge, progress, and performance achievement through learning the basic principles of traditional paper-and-pencil testing methods; performance assessment and authentic assessment; and assessment for learning

(*cont.*)

TABLE 3.1   Assessment courses in Alberta's and Singapore's Higher Education Institutions (adapted from Koh, Lock, Paris, & Niayesh, 2016) (cont.)

Countries/ Institutions	Course/Program/ Year	Objectives	Learning outcomes
	Mastering the Art of Authentic Assessments in M.Ed. Curriculum and Teaching	To provide inservice teachers with different authentic assessment tools for assessing students' deep understanding and other higher-order thinking skills	– To learn about the differences between assessment and measurement/testing – To master the conceptual and theoretical knowledge about authentic assessment – To learn authentic assessment task design and rubric development
	Assessment and Learning in M.Ed. Policy and Management	To enhance policy leaders' understanding of the trends and confluence of assessment and learning	– To understand the principles of assessment for learning – To understand the principles of assessment of learning – To understand the trends and confluence of assessment and learning

(cont.)

TABLE 3.1 Assessment courses in Alberta's and Singapore's Higher Education Institutions (adapted from Koh, Lock, Paris, & Niayesh, 2016) (cont.)

Countries/ Institutions	Course/Program/ Year	Objectives	Learning outcomes
	Assessment for Learning in Master of Teaching	To enable teachers to gain an understanding of formative assessment practices that will help inform instruction and student learning	– To gain knowledge of effective formative assessment practices for the classroom – To understand the importance of instructional alignment within elements of the curriculum; outcomes, content, process, assessment and evaluation – To understand assessment design that enhances the potential for formative assessment practice – To understand the fundamentals of formative assessment theory and apply informed feedback practices on students' work – To address tensions between assessment and learning agendas in the assessment of, for, and as learning discourses

Most of the course outlines in the various master's programs at the University of Calgary and the Nanyang Technological University Singapore were designed and written by the first author of this book. As for other higher education institutions, the course objectives and learning outcomes were extracted from their websites.

As seen in Table 3.1, the three research-intensive universities in Alberta have developed and offered assessment courses in both preservice and inservice teacher education programs. Likewise, assessment courses were offered at both teacher education levels at NIE, the sole teacher training institute in Singapore. Taken together, this indicates the intentional effort of the teacher education programs to provide those designing, developing, and leading curriculum and assessments with rigorous and high-quality assessment education, given global trends in curriculum and assessment reforms. To support the provision of assessment curriculum in teacher education programs, the Alberta Assessment Consortium, an alliance of stakeholders, has played a significant role in developing online assessment resources and workshops for teachers across the province. Most workshops were one-off sessions that featured world-renowned or seasoned speakers in classroom assessment. Despite the termination of AISI, many schools in Alberta have continued school-based professional learning communities with assessment foci.

Countries around the world are amazed by Singaporean students' successes in international assessments. When Finnish students ranked first in PISA, initially launched in 2000, other countries including the US, Canada, and Singapore tried to learn from the Finns' education system. Pasi Sahlberg's (2011) book, *Finnish Lessons: What Can the World Learn from Educational Change in Finland*, became a sensation among policymakers, educational researchers, and educators keen to learn about the successes of educational change in Finland. According to Sahlberg (2011), high-quality teacher education, the high prestige of teaching professionals, low-stakes assessments, and assessment for learning were touted as the key determinants of Finnish students' stellar performance in PISA.

Policymakers, educational researchers, and teacher educators in Singapore worked collaboratively in the process of improving the quality of students' learning through evidence-based research, teacher preparation and professional development programs focusing on transforming teachers' pedagogical and assessment practices. In response to global education reforms, NIE launched the Teacher Education Model for the 21st Century (TE21) in 2009 as "a transformative endeavor that will guide the design, delivery and evaluation of NIE's programs in order to provide the best education to [Singapore's] aspiring and serving teachers to become 21st century teaching professionals"

(NIE, 2009, p. 22). An ultimate goal of the model was to develop teachers' capacity to use innovative pedagogical and assessment methods to educate and nurture students holistically. High-quality education should provide every student with an equitable opportunity to develop morally, intellectually, physically, socially, and emotionally. These various aspects of development correspond to the MOE's Framework for 21st Century Competencies and Student Outcomes, which aims to prepare Singaporean students with the knowledge, skills, and dispositions/attributes needed for their successes as individuals, members of the community, and citizens in an increasingly complex competitive global economy.

Assessment literacy is deemed to be one of the essential outcomes for preservice and inservice teachers enrolled in the teacher preparation program and graduate courses at NIE. Teachers' mastery of a wide repertoire of assessment methods complements the range of innovative pedagogical practices desired in the TE21 model. As such, assessment coursework is intentionally embedded in both teaching and method courses at both preservice and inservice levels. At the program level, e-portfolios are introduced as an assessment of preservice teachers' professional competences. Such an assessment method empowers teachers to be reflective practitioners from the beginning of their candidature through to the end of the practicum.

Recommendations for Teacher Preparation and Professional Development

This chapter presents a tale of two education systems engaged in the pursuit of developing teachers' assessment literacy for the good of their students, given the global education reforms that place greater emphasis on developing students' competencies for their successes in future life and the workplace. We hope that developing teachers' assessment literacy will no longer be primarily rhetoric for educational research and teacher education. Although a substantial body of literature has focused on the importance of developing teachers' assessment literacy through high-quality professional development (e.g., Harlen, 2010; Klinger, Volante, & DeLuca, 2012; Koh, 2011; McMunn, McColskey, & Butler, 2004; Sato, Wei, & Darling-Hammond, 2008; Shepard et al., 2005; Stiggins, 1995), until recently little attention had been given to moving beyond the conceptualization to incorporating the design and implementation of high-quality assessment curriculum for preservice teacher preparation programs.

Below are recommendations for improving the quality of assessment coursework in preservice teacher preparation:

First, teacher educators need to design and implement high-quality assessment coursework intentionally. The focus of the assessment curriculum needs to extend beyond preservice teachers' surface learning of assessment knowledge and principles; teacher educators must create opportunities for preservice teachers to engage in reflective thinking about assessment practices and challenge their prior conceptions of assessment and beliefs about student learning (Koh & Tan, 2016).

Second, according to Darling-Hammond and Snyder (2000), a growing number of teacher preparation programs are using authentic assessments of teaching in which preservice teachers or novice teachers are given the opportunity to develop and understand their "thinking and actions in situations that are experience-based and problem-oriented and that include simulated or actual acts of teaching" (p. 524). This is akin to Lee Shulman's (2005) signature pedagogies, defined as "the types of teaching that organize the fundamental ways in which future practitioners are educated for their new professions" (p. 52). New or novice teachers need to be educated in critical aspects of the three fundamental dimensions of professional work: to think, perform, and act with integrity. Learning to teach requires new teachers and student teachers not only to think like a teacher but also to perform and act as a teacher (Darling-Hammond, 2006). The author of this chapter, Koh (2014b) adopted problem-based learning (PBL) as a signature pedagogy for designing and developing an assessment course implemented in a preservice teacher preparation program at a research-intensive Canadian university (see Koh, 2014b; Koh & Tan, 2016, for details). The course consisted of multiple sections in which student teachers' learning of educational assessment was facilitated by their respective instructors using PBL. As a learner-centered approach, PBL aims to develop not only preservice teachers' assessment literacy but also their critical thinking, complex problem-solving, communication, collaboration, and self-directed learning. If teacher educators envision that these 21st-century competencies are important for K–12 students, then preservice teachers need to be able to demonstrate these competencies prior to their entry into actual classrooms. This will enable them to adopt learner-centered pedagogical approaches and assessment methods to develop their students' competencies.

In a typical PBL lesson, preservice teachers work in small groups first and then individually to solve contextualized, ill-structured problems embedded within the assessment tasks (i.e., authentic assessments) as the primary pathway of learning. The problems are complex and rooted in real-world situations and designed to reflect a typical problem (e.g., assessment balance, assessment for learning), encountered by teaching professionals worldwide. In the context of the assessment course, teacher educators model PBL, authentic assessment, and assessment for learning to preservice teachers and demonstrate how these innovative pedagogical and assessment methods can be used to enhance K–12 students' learning experiences and to promote their mastery of disciplinary knowledge and 21st-century competencies.

Third, it is important for teacher preparation programs to partner with K–12 schools to promote preservice teachers' extensive observation of strategies and actively try out new pedagogical approaches and assessment methods they have learned from their coursework. Oftentimes, preservice teachers learn from their partner or mentor teachers during practicums. Many preservice teachers may not be able or will be reluctant to translate what they have learned from an assessment course unless they have received continuing support from their field supervisors and partner teachers. An understanding of the theory-practice nexus is key to increasing preservice teachers' willingness to adopt and implement new pedagogical approaches and assessment methods. Hence, it is vital to ensure a comprehensive integration between coursework and supervised field experience for preservice teachers.

Fourth, preservice teachers need to pursue a career-long commitment to professional learning and growth in assessment. Professional learning opportunities can extend beyond formal assessment courses in undergraduate teacher preparation programs. There are many ways for preservice teachers to develop their assessment literacy at different career stages, for example, summer institutes, workshops, seminars, and conferences. For example, Koh and Chapman (2017) have explored the design and implementation of authentic assessment learning activities through two summer institutes to build preservice elementary teachers' capacity in mathematics authentic assessment. Koh and Chapman's research is funded by the Social Sciences and Humanities Research Council of Canada.

Given that there has been a substantial body of research on inservice teacher professional learning, the recommendations for the design of teacher professional development programs are intentionally brief:

First, it is important to conduct a needs analysis of teachers prior to the design, development, and implementation of professional development workshops or programs. This is because inservice teachers may not have the same entry levels of assessment knowledge and skills. Thus, professional development workshops need to be adaptable. It is also necessary to provide teachers with the opportunity to reflect on their conceptions of the purposes and functions of assessment. The research on teachers' beliefs and conceptions clearly demonstrates that teachers' conceptions of assessment are influenced by their educational experiences, sociocultural backgrounds, and the larger political environment (Brown, 2011). It is well established that teachers' ideas and beliefs are strongly influenced by their earlier educational experiences as students (Pajares, 1992).

Guskey (2002) shows that the effects of school-based professional development on teachers' changes in classroom practices are mediated by teachers' prior notions or beliefs. Thus, developing teachers' assessment literacy through professional development that focuses on teachers' knowledge and skills in designing new forms of assessment is a necessary precursor, but not sufficient to ensure subsequent changes in teachers' assessment practices. Hargreaves, Earl, and Schmidt (2002), for instance, contend that alternative assessment reform (i.e., implementation of authentic assessment and assessment for learning) needs to be understood from a "cultural perspective." This means it is necessary for the workshop facilitator to conduct an investigation of how teachers rethink or re-conceptualize the nature and purposes of classroom assessment within their specific sociocultural contexts. A cultural perspective also suggests an imperative to understand the fundamental assumptions that underpin the teachers' conceptions of assessment rather than assume that there is likely to be a direct change in teachers' assessment practices after their participation in professional development programs or workshops. Oftentimes, teachers may simply and routinely apply what they have learned from professional development experiences, or they may uphold conventional assessment practices, depending upon their own perceptions of the value and merit of assessment.

Additionally, a common challenge many teachers face is time constraints. Hence, school-based professional learning communities (PLCs) in assessment must be designed and implemented to provide inservice teachers with high-quality assessment content, learning materials, and resources. According to Hargreaves and Fullan (2012), some PLCs have a tendency to "stick to the technicalities of specifying narrow performance goals, defining a focus, examining data, and establishing teams" (p. 129). In addition, the design and implementation of PLCs need to include teachers' voices, in meaningful ways, so they feel they have the autonomy to define the learning goals of PLCs. Sumara and Davis's (2009) study, for example, shows that many of the school-based PLCs spearheaded by school leaders in Alberta's AISI initiatives failed to produce deep change in school cultures, due to the imposition of top-down policies. This indicates the importance of encouraging teachers' bottom-up initiatives so PLCs are representative of their views in addressing students' learning needs.

These recommendations are not exhaustive, but they arise out of an endeavor to explore and present a tale of two education systems which represent two different cultural contexts (i.e., east versus west) and are constantly surrounded by a sea change in educational policies due to global reforms. As we move forward, preservice teacher preparation and inservice teacher professional development programs are expected to play an increasingly pivotal role to explore richer and authentic professional learning experiences for teacher candidates as well as new and experienced teachers in a complex, competitive world. Developing teachers' assessment literacy should neither be a rhetorical nor a one-off event. Instead, we teacher educators need to provide continuing support for teachers to develop a growth mindset and inculcate lifelong learning habits in them if we envision them transforming their instructional and assessment practices.

Note

1 These competencies also include the non-cognitive dispositions and values that are recommended by the PERI and SERI committees.

References

Alberta Education. (2010). *Inspiring education: A dialogue with Albertans.* Retrieved from https://open.alberta.ca/dataset/45370ce9-3a90-4ff2-8735-cdb760c720f0/resource/2ee2452c-81d3-414f-892f-060caf40e78e/download/4492270-2010-inspiring-education-dialogue-albertans-2010-04.pdf

Alberta Education. (2011). *Framework for student learning: Competencies for engaged thinkers and ethical citizens with an entrepreneurial spirit.* Alberta. Retrieved from http://globeclassroom.ca/userfiles/Alberta_Framework.pdf

Alberta Education. (2016). *The guiding framework for the design and development of kindergarten to grade 12 provincial curriculum (Programs of Study).* Retrieved from https://education.alberta.ca/media/3575996/curriculum-development-guiding-framework.pdf

Alberta Government. (2018). *Alberta education teaching quality standard.* Retrieved from https://education.alberta.ca/media/3739620/standardsdoc-tqs-_fa-web-2018-01-17.pdf

AISI Education Partners. (2008). *Alberta initiative for school improvement: AISI handbook for cycle 4, 2009–2012.* Retrieved from http://www.assembly.ab.ca/lao/library/egovdocs/2008/aled/173449.pdf

Auguste, B., Kihn, P., & Miller, M. (2010). *Closing the talent gap: Attracting and retaining top-third graduates to careers in teaching: An international and market research-based perspective.* London: McKinsey and Company.

Barber, M., & Mourshed, M. (2007). *How the world's best-performing school systems come out on top*. London: McKinsey and Company.

Bennett, D. (2016, June 15). Alberta announces sweeping 6-year overhaul of school curricula at cost of $64M. *Global News*. Retrieved from https://globalnews.ca/news/2764146/alberta-announces-sweeping-6-year-overhaul-of-school-curricula-at-cost-of-64m/

Black, P., & Wiliam, D. (1998a). Inside the black box: Raising standards through classroom assessment. *Phi Delta Kappan, 80*, 139–148.

Black, P., & Wiliam, D. (1998b). Assessment and classroom learning. *Assessment in Education: Principles, Policy & Practice, 5*(1), 7–74.

Brown, G. T. L. (2011). Teachers' conceptions of assessment: Comparing primary and secondary teachers in New Zealand. *Assessment Matters, 3*, 45–70.

CMEC. (2012). *Measuring up: Canadian results of the OECD PISA study*. Toronto: Council of Ministers of Education, Canada.

CMEC. (2015). *Measuring up: Canadian results of the OECD PISA study: The performance of Canada's youth in science, reading, and mathematics*. Toronto: Council of Ministers of Education, Canada.

Crocker, R. (2009). Rethinking the AISI research model: Secondary data analysis and future applications. In A. Hargreaves, R. Crocker, B. Davis, L. McEwen, P. Sahlberg, D. Shirley, & D. Sumara (Eds.), *The learning mosaic: A multiple perspectives review of the Alberta Initiative for School Improvement (AISI)* (pp. 9–33). Edmonton: Alberta Education.

Darling-Hammond, L. (2006). Constructing 21st-century teacher education. *Journal of Teacher Education, 57*(X), 1–15.

Darling-Hammond, L., & Adamson, F. (2010). *Beyond basic skills: The role of performance assessment in achieving 21st century standards of learning*. Stanford, CA: Stanford University, Stanford Center for Opportunity Policy in Education. Retrieved from https://scale.stanford.edu/system/files/beyond-basic-skills-role-performance-assessment-achieving-21st-century-standards-learning.pdf

Darling-Hammond, L., & Snyder, J. (2000). Authentic assessment of teaching in context. *Teaching and Teacher Education, 16*(5–6), 523–545.

Earl, L. (2003). *Assessment as learning: Using classroom assessment to maximize student learning*. Thousand Oaks, CA: Corwin Press.

Goh, C. B., & Gopinathan, S. (2008). The development of education in Singapore since 1965. In S. K. Lee, C. B. Goh, B. Fredriksen, & J. P. Tan (Eds.), *Toward a better future: Education and training for economic development in Singapore since 1965* (pp. 12–38). Washington, DC: The World Bank.

Goodwin, A. L. (2012). Quality teachers, Singapore style. In L. Darling-Hammond & A. Lieberman (Eds.), *Teacher education around the world* (pp. 22–43). New York, NY: Taylor & Francis.

Goodwin, A. L., Low, E. L., & Darling-Hammond, L. (2017). *Empowered educators in Singapore: How high-performing systems shape teaching quality*. San Francisco, CA: Jossey-Bass.

Guskey, T. R. (2002). Professional development and teacher change. *Teachers & Teaching, 8*(3–4), 381–391.

Hargreaves, A., Crocker, R., Davis, B., McEwen, L., Sahlberg, P., Shirley, D., & Sumara, D. (2009). *The learning mosaic: A multiple perspectives review of the Alberta Initiative for School Improvement (AISI)*. Edmonton: Alberta Education.

Hargreaves, A., Earl, L., & Schmidt, M. (2002). Perspectives on alternative assessment reform. *American Educational Research Journal, 39*(1), 69–95.

Hargreaves, A., & Fullan, M. (2012). *Professional capital: Transforming teaching in every school*. New York, NY: Teachers College Press.

Harlen, W. (2010). What is quality teacher assessment. In J. Gardner, W. Harlen, L. Hayward, & G. Stobart (Eds.), *Developing teacher assessment* (pp. 29–52). Maidenhead: Open University Press.

Hiebert, J., & Stigler, J. W. (2017). Teaching versus teachers as a lever for change: Comparing a Japanese and a U.S. perspective on improving instruction. *Educational Researcher, 46*(4), 169–176.

Hodge, K. A., & Lear, J. L. (2011). Employment skills for 21st century workplace: The gap between faculty and student perceptions. *Journal of Career and Technical Education, 26*(2), 28–41.

Klinger, D. A., Volante, L., & DeLuca, C. (2012). Building teacher capacity within the evolving assessment culture in Canadian Education. *Policy Futures in Education, 10*(4), 447–460.

Koh, K. (2011). Improving teachers' assessment literacy through professional development. *Teaching Education, 22*(3), 255–276.

Koh, K. (2014a). Authentic assessment, teacher judgment and moderation in a context of high accountability. In C. Wyatt-Smith, V. Klenowski, & P. Colbert (Eds.), *Designing assessment for quality learning: The enabling power of assessment* (Vol. 1, pp. 249–264). Dordrecht: Springer.

Koh, K. (2014b). Developing pre-service teachers' assessment literacy: A problem-based learning approach. In P. Preciado Babb (Ed.), *Proceedings of the IDEAS rising to the challenge* (pp. 113–120). Calgary: Werklund School of Education, University of Calgary.

Koh, K. (2017). Authentic assessment. *Oxford Research Encyclopedia of Education*. New York, NY: Oxford University Press.

Koh, K., Burke, L. E. C., Luke, A., Gong, W. G., & Tan, C. (2017). Developing the assessment literacy of teachers in Chinese language classrooms: A focus on assessment task design. *Language Teaching Research*. doi:10.1177/1362168816684366

Koh, K., & Chapman, O. (2017, June). *Supporting preservice mathematics teachers' development of knowledge of authentic assessment tasks*. Paper presented at the Canadian Society for the Study of Education. Toronto, ON: Ryerson University.

Koh, K., Lock, J., Paris, B., & Niayesh, M. (2016). Building Canadian preservice teachers' capacity in classroom assessment. In M. Hirschkorn & J. Mueller (Eds.), *What should Canada's teachers know? Teachers' capacities: knowledge, beliefs, and skills* (pp. 72–98). Ottawa: Canadian Association for Teacher Education.

Koh, K., & Luke, A. (2009). Authentic and conventional assessment in Singapore schools: An empirical study of teacher assignments and student work. *Assessment in Education: Principles, Policy & Practice, 16*(3), 291–318.

Koh, K., & Tan, C. (2016). Promoting reflection in pre-service teachers through problem-based learning: An example from Canada. *Reflective Practice, 17*(3), 347–356.

Low, E. L., Goodwin, A., & Snyder, J. (2017). *Focused on learning: Student and teacher time in a Singapore school*. Stanford, CA: Stanford Center for Opportunity Policy in Education.

Luke, A. (2011). Generalizing across borders: Policy and the limits of educational science. *Educational Researcher, 40*(8), 367–377.

McMunn, N., McColskey, W., & Butler, S. (2004). Building teacher capacity in classroom assessment to improve student learning. *International Journal of Educational Policy, Research, & Practice, 4*(4), 25–28.

Ministry of Education. (2009a). *Report of the primary education review and implementation committee*. Singapore: Ministry of Education.

Ministry of Education. (2009b). *Framework for 21st century competencies and student outcomes*. Retrieved from https://www.moe.gov.sg/education/education-system/21st-century-competencies

Ministry of Education. (2010). *Report of the secondary review and implementation committee*. Singapore: Ministry of Education.

National Academy of Engineering and National Research Council. (2014). *STEM integration in K–12 education: Status, prospects, and an agenda for research*. Washington, DC: The National Academic Press.

National Institute of Education. (2009). *TE21: A teacher education model for the 21st century*. Singapore: National Institute of Education.

Newmann, F. M., Bryk, A. S., & Nagaoka, J. K. (2001). *Authentic intellectual work and standardized tests: Conflict or coexistence? Improving Chicago's Schools*. Chicago, IL: Consortium on Chicago School Research.

Newmann, F. M., Marks, H. M., & Gamoran, A. (1996). Authentic pedagogy and student performance. *American Journal of Education, 104*, 280–312.

OECD. (2012). *PISA 2009 technical report*. Paris: PISA, OECD Publishing. Retrieved from http://dx.doi.org/10.1787/9789264167872-en

Ong, Y. K. (2018, September 2018). *Opening address of the Minister for Education:* Learn for life (Schools Work Plan Seminar). Singapore: Ministry of Education. Retrieved from https://www.moe.gov.sg/news/speeches/opening-address-by-mr-ong-ye-kung--minister-for-education--at-the-schools-work-plan-seminar

Pajares, M. F. (1992). Teachers' beliefs and educational research: Cleaning up a messy construct. *Review of Educational Research, 62*(3), 307–332.

Parsons, J., & Hewson, K. (2014). How did AISI advance the work of school principals? *ATA Magazine, 94*(4), 5–9. Retrieved from https://www.teachers.ab.ca/News%20Room/ata%20magazine/Volume-94/Number-4/Pages/How-did-AISI-advance-the-work-of-school-principals.aspx

Partnership for 21st Century Skills. (2002). *Learning for the 21st century skills: A report and MLE guide on 21st century skills.* Retrieved from http://www.p21.org/storage/documents/P21_Report.pdf

Partnership for 21st Century Skills. (2008). *21st Century skills, education & competitiveness: A resource and policy guide.* Tucson: Partnership for 21st Century Skills. Retrieved from http://www.p21.org/documents/21st_century_skills_education_and_competitiveness_guide.pdf

Robelen, E. (2011, January 26). *Obama emphasizes STEM education in state of the union.* Retrieved from http://blogs.edweek.org/edweek/curriculum/2011/01/obama_laments_quality_of_us_ma.html

Rotherham, A. J., & Willingham, D. (2009). 21st century skills: The challenges ahead. *Educational Leadership, 67*(1), 16–21.

Sahlberg, P. (2011). *Finnish lessons: What can the world learn from educational change in Finland?* New York, NY: Teachers' College.

Sato, M., Wei, R. C., & Darling-Hammond, L. (2008). Improving teachers' assessment practices through professional development: The case of National Board Certification. *American Educational Research Journal, 45*(3), 669–700.

Shanmugaratnam, T. (2005, September 22). *MOE Work Plan Seminar 2005.* Retrieved from https://www.moe.gov.sg/media/speeches/2005/sp20050922.htm

Shepard, L. (2000). The role of assessment in a learning culture. *Educational Researcher, 29*(7), 4–14.

Shepard, L., Hammerness, K., Darling-Hammond, L., Rust, F., Baratz Snowden, J., Gordon, E., ... Pacheco, A. (2005). In L. Darling-Hammond & J. Bransford (Eds.), *Preparing teachers for a changing world* (pp. 275–326). San Francisco, CA: John Wiley.

Shulman, L. S. (2005). Signature pedagogies in the professions. *Daedalus, 134*(3), 52–59.

Song, E., & Koh, K. (2010). *Assessment for learning: Understanding teachers' beliefs and practices.* Proceedings of the International Association for Educational Assessment (IAEA) 36th Annual Conference, Bangkok, Thailand.

Stiggins, R. J. (1995). Assessment literacy for the 21st century. *Phi Delta Kappan, 77*(3), 238–245.

Stiggins, R. J. (2002). Assessment crisis: The absence of assessment for learning. *Phi Delta Kappan, 83*(10), 758–765.

Sumara, D., & Davis, B. (2009). Using complexity science to study the impact of AISI on cultures of education in Alberta. In A. Hargreaves, R. Crocker, B. Davis, L. McEwen, P. Sahlberg, D. Shirley, ... D. Sumara (Eds.), *The learning mosaic: A multiple perspectives review of the Alberta Initiative for School Improvement (AISI)* (pp. 34–50). Edmonton: Alberta Education.

Tan, C. (2008). Globalization, the Singapore state and educational reforms: Towards performativity. *Education, Knowledge & Economy, 2*(2), 1–24.

Tan, C., Koh, K., & Choy, K. (2016). *The education system in Singapore*. In S. Juszczyk (Ed.), *Asian education systems* (pp. 129–148). Poland: Publishing House Adam Marszalek.

The Economist Intelligence Unit. (2018). *The global liveability index 2018: A free overview*. Retrieved from https://pages.eiu.com/rs/753-RIQ-438/images/The_Global_Liveability_Index_2018.pdf

Theobald C. (2015, March 13). Fraser report: New learning assessments focus on students' needs. *Edmonton Sun*. Retrieved from https://edmontonsun.com/2015/03/13/fraser-report-new-learning-assessments-focus-on-students-needs/wcm/48a5fc5f-149d-4007-9e56-00d6f3c27cea

Wiggins, G. (1989). A true test: Toward more authentic and equitable assessment. *Phi Delta Kappan, 70*, 703–713.

CHAPTER 4

Designing Teacher Education to Promote the Love of Wisdom within a Competency-Based Assessment System

Sean Steel

Introduction: The Trend toward Marginalizing Philosophy

Philosophy of education or education foundations is not regularly offered as a core course in most B. Ed. PBL programs today. The eradication of philosophy of education from teacher's colleges stems, in part, from a lack of vision, courage, and understanding among the elites who develop such professional programs, but also from general impatience with philosophy of education among the tuition-paying "clientele" who attend teacher's colleges to earn their teaching certifications and obtain well-paying teaching positions. Such students are almost invariably focused on whatever is the most efficient means of gaining employment, of developing career competence and career success. They ordinarily come to education programs demanding a toolbox of teaching ideas, solutions, techniques, and approaches. Students of the present day demand diagnostic checklists and manuals they think will unlock for them the ostensible secrets of how to be good teachers and assessors. They expect to leave their teacher's colleges with all the requisite knowledge, skills, attributes, and competencies. And, of course, they want all of this to happen within two years if they have the first degree.

Philosophy of education is not really concerned with such things, however, and for many students, it does not seem to relate to their career imperatives. Certainly, shrewd philosophy of education course designers and book developers will always try to make it appear as though philosophy serves these lesser concerns, but this approach is disingenuous and misleading since it tends to sideline what philosophy (as the practice "loving wisdom") truly is. For instance, in post-secondary institutions where philosophy of education has not yet been entirely eliminated from study, it is common to organize student learning by adopting one of two approaches. First, a philosophy of education instructor might opt to organize a course as a broad survey in the History of Educational Philosophy using a textbook like Nel Noddings' popular *Philosophy of Education* (Westview Press, 2012). Second, an alternative to this *survey-based* approach is an issues-based design where student-teachers will read a problem-themed textbook like Richard Bailey's edited compilation, *The Philosophy of Education: An Introduction* (Continuum, 2010). In either case, it is not difficult to link excerpted readings and formal academic work to specific B.Ed. program knowledge, goals, or outcomes as well as to broader, stipulated competencies. With either, the spirit of philosophy and philosophizing is not placed at the center of course design; so, the precious opportunity to have student-teachers genuinely experiment with wisdom-seeking is lost.

Moreover, these two contemporary approaches to philosophy of education in B.Ed. programs do not necessarily even protect such courses from the chopping block. First, the pay-off for students who must enroll in such courses seems negligible to them, and they are often vocal about this in negative and derisive course evaluations, of which more land crushingly upon the heads of untenured, low-paid, term-contract instructors. Second, the value of such courses are equally unconvincing to decision-making elites concerned, after all, with the students' acquisition of professional teacher competencies as stipulated by the teaching standards. Philosophy of education or education foundations strikes them as suspiciously inept and *passé regarding practical accomplishments.* For, on the one hand, philosophy of education is unconcerned with the technical delivery of curriculum design skills, or knowledge in the nuts and bolts of daily lesson planning. It likewise eschews any associations with the diagnostic toolbox aspects of teacher preparation. On the other hand, philosophy of education also seems less able to provide any of the goods one might cultivate efficiently, simply by fragmenting the B.Ed. curriculum into a broad variety of specialized courses that provide diverse lenses through which to study complex educational phenomena. In Canada, such courses include educational leadership, educational psychology, educational technology, literacy, numeracy, special education, English Language Learning (ELL), previously English as a Second Language, STEM (Science, Technology, Engineering, and Mathematics), curriculum design, educational assessment, LGBTQ (Lesbian, Gay, Bisexual, Transsexual and Queer education), and FNMI (First Nations, Métis, and Indigenous education), to name a few., Other than the lip-service paid to philosophy at the end of their degrees when all student-teachers must craft a so-called philosophy of teaching statement they might use for job applications, philosophy of education is altogether crowded out in B. Ed. programming. Teacher education nowadays supposes that the genuine heart of education is concerned with demonstrating career competencies. Philosophy of education, properly understood, makes no such assumption.

The Competencies Movement and Its Impact on Teacher Education

There is a disconnect between competency-based education and a deeper form of education that concerns itself with wisdom-seeking, or philosophy. In my home province of Alberta, Canada, for instance, all B. Ed. students must, by Ministerial Order #016/97, demonstrate their competence in relation to a broad array of interim indicators for requisite knowledge, skills, and attributes (KSA's); likewise, professional teachers must meet an equally extensive number of KSA benchmarks to gain permanent certification within the province. This outcome-based teacher assessment arrangement has recently been updated so that by September 1, 2019, the long list of 28 KSA's enumerated in the 1997 Ministerial Order will be reduced to a total of six over-arching competencies. As of March 2016, the Alberta Government's draft *Teaching Quality Standard* (TQS) listed these as follows:

> (i) Engaging in Career-Long Learning, (ii) Demonstrating a Professional Body of Knowledge, (iii) Fostering Effective Relationships, (iv) Establishing Inclusive Learning Environments, (v) Applying Foundational Knowledge about First Nations, Metis, and Inuit, and (vi) Adhering to Legal Frameworks and Policies. (Government of Alberta, 2016)

So, what is the difference between the previous KSA/outcomes-based system and the new competencies-based system? To start, it is important to note that there is no singular definition of competency in the literature, perhaps because a wide variety of stakeholders in education view competency in many ways (Hoffmann, 1999). Nonetheless, in Alberta, the new TQS document defines a competency as "an interrelated set of knowledge, skills and attitudes, developed over time and drawn upon and applied to a particular teaching context in order to support optimum student learning as required by the *Teaching Quality Standard* statement" (Government of Alberta, 2016; Government of Alberta, 2018). In this example, we see how the definition of competency is relativized to suit the specific educational concerns of the accrediting administrative body. For a simpler perspective about competencies, however, we might turn to an international source for a definition offered by the National Post-secondary Education Cooperative (NPEC) Working Group on Competency-Based Initiatives in Post-secondary Education. They define competency as "the combination of skills, abilities, and knowledge needed to perform a specific task" (Jones & Voorhees, 2002, p. 7). In the NPEC Report, Jones and Voorhees remark that competencies result from "integrative learning experiences in which skills, abilities, and knowledge interact to form bundles that have currency in relation to tasks for which they are assembled" (p. 7). At the heart of ideas about competence, then, is the acknowledgment that in assessing professional competencies, the ability to perform specific tasks is pivotal (Drisko, 2014, p. 416). As assessable, task-related, external behaviors, competencies should always concern "a dimension of behavior that is relevant to performance in the job." As Charles Woodruffe (1993) remarked, "Competencies are behavioral repertoires that some people carry out better than others." In his view, these behavioral dimensions should be the focus of job analyses (p. 29).

The entire foundation of the worldwide competencies movement (as expressed in statements like those of Drisko, 2014; Jones & Voorhees, 2002; Woodruffe, 1993) therefore rests upon the notion of education as means toward a job or career qualification. Naturally enough, competencies within different job contexts require different bundles or clusters of skills and knowledge. It is precisely this bundling and unbundling that drives competency-based initiatives among post-secondary institutions in this century. From the perspective of those within the competency-based education movement, the challenge "is to determine which competencies can be bundled together to provide which types of learners the optimal combination of skills and knowledge needed to perform a specific task" (Jones & Voorhees, 2002, p. 9). Essentially, then, the competencies model takes away some of the professional flexibility available to assessors under the older KSA system who might have looked for knowledge, skills, and attributes in alternative bundlings perhaps not recognized as legitimate or optimal by elite managerial, administrative, or governing bodies. As we shall see, this focus upon the assessment of career competencies in B.Ed. programs is animated by an anti-philosophic spirit. John Burgoyne (1993) wrote an insightful critique of the drive toward competency-based education. In his view, the general thrust of the competency movement is "that the purposes of development can and should be more tightly defined in relation to work to ensure its relevance and to provide a focus for the efficient management of learning" (Burgoyne, 1993, p. 6). Having carefully studied its historical context, Burgoyne's suspicions were raised, wherein he stated that "it is tempting to interpret the competence movement as a return to a concern for control in society and to be part of a broader pattern" (Burgoyne, p. 6).

Certainly, there is something in the drive toward prefabricated, assessment-ready bundlings that smacks of narrowed educational horizons and possibilities. As Burgoyne observed, the competency-focused paradigm of education "seeks to impose an overly simple model on the complexity of the occupational, organizational, training, education and development world, given the range of issues which are involved in its theory and practice" (1993, p. 7).

Concerning this reductionist view of post-secondary education as a matter of job accreditation, other scholars who have studied the competency movement have likewise written that "Post-secondary education has become progressively responsive to the needs of business and industry, where learning is closely tied to competencies and performance-based assessment of those competencies" (Baughman, 2012, p. 25; Gardner, 2009). Indeed, since the 1990s, "competencies have become code words for the human resources and strategic management practices of recruiting, selecting, placing, leading, and training employees and evaluating employee performance" (Baughman, Brumm, & Mickelson, 2012, p. 116).

More can be said about the constricted, managerial view of teachers strictly as education workers and career professionals. Of particular note is how this view of education marks such a departure from the long-standing, traditional Western understanding of education where higher education was always, in some fashion, related to a genuinely liberal education. Whether we are speaking of its ancient Pythagorean roots, whether we refer to the classical trivium of grammar, rhetoric, and dialectics, alongside the quadrivium of arithmetic, music, geometry, and astronomy, or whether we consider its more modern iterations, liberal education has always concerned liberating the human spirit from itself—that is, from its own egoistic concerns, from all of its fixations extraneous to study, including petty cares about utility, productivity, assessments and evaluations, and career application. A liberal education, classically-understood, has always been a kind of transformative enterprise designed to elevate and challenge the mind and emancipate the spirit from the chains otherwise imposed upon it by those demanding relevance, accountability, and competence in all things related to a workaday existence.

If we look to the silences and what has been left out in B.Ed. programs where competency-based course designs reign supreme, we will happily stumble upon the lost, forgotten, and most precious meanings of both philosophy and teaching. In the present day, instructors have adopted the mandated, hegemonic paradigm for relevance successfully promulgated by elites in the competency movement. By resigning themselves to cultivating and demonstrating career competencies to remain viable minor components in B.Ed. programs, instructors who teach courses in philosophy of education, education theory, or education foundations have done much to undermine and eradicate the precious contribution that wisdom-seeking practices might otherwise make in the lives of teachers and students. Simply put: they have misportrayed the central meaning and identity of philosophy by treating it as though it were meant to be a handmaiden for banausic competencies. They have likewise adopted a second falsehood fundamental to the competency movement itself: they have swallowed the assumption that teaching is just a professional career or job like any other. Both impressions are gravely mistaken, and they threaten to tear out the precious heart of both teaching and education philosophy. But all is not lost. There is a third way. This happy alternative mode of designing instruction that incorporates authentic philosophy of education at the center is the subject of the remainder of this chapter.

The Third Way: Making Philosophy of Education Core to Pedagogy

The pedagogical approaches that marginalize transformative intellectual activity in favor of competency acquisition as discussed above are not the only avenues for locating philosophy of education in preservice teacher preparation. There is a third, ancient, way that has mostly been lost, but that is intimately associated with the original meaning of philosophy, as well as with the deep heart of teaching practice.

The third way of approaching philosophy has been referenced and promoted by a number of esteemed scholars including Pierre Hadot (1995, 2002), Algis Uzdavinys (2004, 2008, 2011), Josef Pieper (1992, 1998, 2008), and Peter Kingsley (1995, 1998, 2003), to name a few. My advocacy for this third way of approaching philosophizing with students is therefore not novel or without a credible pedigree. Indeed, if there is anything innovative in the following discussion, it is not that I have taken up this lost, core meaning of philosophy, but that I have endeavored to do so in the context of a professional B.Ed. degree program dominated by concerns about competency-based assessment.

Let us commence thinking about this third way by inquiring briefly into the ancient Greek meaning of philosophy as the love of wisdom. We begin by acknowledging that wisdom (*sophia*) is the greatest and most precious good. Indeed, it is that good without which no other goods can be truly enjoyed; all others are ambiguous in value. Further, we must recognize that philosophy, or the love of wisdom, is a way of life according to all of its ancient practitioners. It is not a course of study, methodology, or subject you might either pick up or put aside. Having a Ph.D. in philosophy does not make you a philosopher, either. Rather, philosophy is a kind of spirit that must inhabit you on a daily, even moment-to-moment, basis. It involves the mindful cultivation of our yearning for this one Greatest Good (*Summum Bonum*). Its pursuit requires learning to relax from all other lesser goods, including our own egos. This is why Plato called philosophy the "art of dying." If what I am saying about philosophy is unclear, please do not be discouraged or feel threatened. It calls for contemplative practice to be understood.

In his *Nicomachean Ethics,* Aristotle tells us that there is both an active and a contemplative component to this way of life. The contemplative aspect involves us in seeking to know the truth about what Josef Pieper calls "the totality of things" (Pieper, 1992). Philosophy is, therefore, a deeply spiritual practice of inquiry. It erupts from the heart of our intimately human desire to know; it activates our most sublime qualities, and it connects us with what is the most sublime aim of our knowing. We are fortunate to encounter the spirit of philosophy in our lives, and it is a shame when we make no space for it, or toss it aside as though it were of no account to us.

But there is also, says Aristotle, an active aspect to the philosophic life. This element is manifest when we seek to know the truth about being (*ousia*) in concert with others: when you and I, in the spirit of wisdom-seeking, invite others to engage with us in wisdom's pursuit, when we put our own private interests and ego concerns aside, and when we cultivate our attentiveness and consciousness to be receptive toward this grand vision (*theoria*) of the common good (*koinon*) together. These two aspects of philosophy, the active and the contemplative, stand together always; as a general rule, if you are rid of the one, you are also rid of the other.

Given this brief gloss on the ancient, original meaning of philosophy, in any activity worthy of the name philosophy, one would therefore expect to find some leadership that renders available the possibility for those involved to experiment with or practice opening themselves to this peculiar spirit of inquiry—and not for the purpose of attaining some number of lower, ambiguous goods enumerated among the requisite knowledge, skills, or attributes for a specific career path, nor as behavioral evidence of competency within a larger bundling of KSAs, but because wisdom is a good to be pursued for its own sake, and without which no amount of competencies in lower things will ever amount to much. Where the first two approaches to philosophy of education already discussed remain oblivious to this larger, lost meaning, this third way does not.

Adopting the third approach to philosophy of education offers the delightful prospect of transformation to those who will take up its challenge sincerely. Pierre Hadot (2002) remarks that, at its origins, philosophy always demanded that its practitioners undergo a personal transformation, or *askesis,* and that this transformation is cultivated both through philosophic discourses as well as by exposure to certain spiritual exercises. In agreement with Hadot, my philosophy of education offerings include readings and exercises for B.Ed. students intended to ensure that all participants are invited to engage experimentally not only in a range of philosophic discourses but also in an array of spiritual exercises associated with philosophy when practiced as a way of life.

Obviously, certain structures need to be in place to help students enter into this experimental mood, including ways to help them be less distracted by their habitual concerns around assessment, grading, and competencies. In the ancient world, such a wisdom-seeking environment was deemed essential to facilitate leisure or *schole*—the Greek term from which we derive our own English word, school. Better than anyone, the ancients knew that the spiritual practice of *schole* must be protected from the banausic (and nowadays hegemonic) demands of those lacking any patience or understanding of its deep value. And today especially, any possibility for genuine school (or *schole*) needs to be preserved from interference by busybodies (*polypragmosynoi*) who are fond of curriculum mapping and rationalizing every learning task in terms of its relevance, program responsibility, ease of assessment, and accountability to the world of work (*ascholia*), with its competency concerns and career-based objectives—all far lesser goods than wisdom. In any philosophy of education course that adopts this third way, the challenge for instructors will be to ensure that students be held accountable for demonstrating core B.Ed. certification competencies, while at the same time carving out a space for them to engage in the wisdom-seeking practices which lay at the heart of genuine *schole*. This can be a difficult balancing act.

Integrating Teaching as a Way of Life

The intimate association between the lost, core meaning of philosophy on the one hand and teaching on the other is not an innovation. Fifteen-hundred years after Aristotle wrote about the active and contemplative aspects of the philosophic life in his *Nicomachean Ethics*, scholastic philosopher Thomas Aquinas pointed out in his *Summa Theologica* how similar the authentic teacher's existence must be to the genuine philosopher's daily life. Put simply, the active and contemplative lives are not just of concern to the philosopher. In Aquinas' view, the teacher most especially must partake in both the active and contemplative aspects of loving wisdom. It may sound ludicrous that our most precious task as teachers is not to teach students literacy or numeracy, nor creative, innovative, technologically savvy decision-making and critical thinking—the very competencies we are expected to teach by our corporate and government administrators. These may be the accountabilities of teaching as a job or profession, but as a way of life, they fall short. Our most solemn endeavor ought rather to be to invite our students into the genuine heart of education, which always must concern wisdom's pursuit.

Understanding this is crucial; where the competency movement treats teaching as though it were simply a professional career path or a job in which proper training means the successful demonstration of specially-formulated bundles of job-related outcomes, thousands of years of philosophic and intellectual tradition should have taught us otherwise. If we only care to look, we can learn that teaching is not a job like any other. Only to the most careless observer does teaching appear to be simply a job. Properly understood, it is a way of life in which both the active and contemplative components must be practiced daily. Without special care and attention to this deep core meaning of teaching, our teacher practice will be empty; all our efforts at educating will be misguided, or at best, of ambiguous value, even having demonstrated all the requisite career competencies.

Having gained this most basic of insights that teaching is a way of life, we find the tables entirely turned on the commonplace dismissal of philosophy of education in B.Ed. programs. Where before it looked as though every other sort of specialized expertise course in an education program was better-suited to educate teachers because of the manner in which each is so carefully tailored to address the core competencies of the teaching profession, now we realize that teaching is, first and foremost, a way of life in which adherents must daily practice and develop its active and contemplative components. Consequently, we now realize that philosophy, as this way of life, provides the very best means of education for teachers who would not only pursue the truth about being (the contemplative aspect of teaching) but who would also lovingly entice their neighbors (i.e., their students) toward this self-same pursuit (its active aspect). Our usual manner of educating in B.Ed. programs is, in light of this ancient insight, entirely backward to what a deeper understanding and appreciation would dictate.

Artful Organization of Philosophy of Education in Competency-Based B.Ed. Learning

The basic curricular challenge in approaching philosophy of education within a B.Ed. program is to ensure that instructors are doing the deep, precious things that promote experimentation with the philosophic spirit while at the same time demonstrating that the design of the course is intelligently connected to cultivating and assessing the core competencies required for teacher certification. For readers interested in cultivating the love of wisdom not only in our own lives as teachers, but also in the lives of our students, and who require a case study or concrete example as guidance and for clarification, a more thorough exposition of my larger philosophy of education designs is now available through Peter Lang Publishing. It is titled *Teacher Education and the Pursuit of Wisdom: A Practical Guide for Education Philosophy Courses*. In the remainder of this chapter, however, you will find a brief description of some key ideas, assessment tools, and organizational structures I have found helpful in tackling the particular problem of planning for philosophy of education in a competency-based B.Ed. program.

The focus throughout the philosophy of education courses I have developed has been on learning to see: to see ourselves, to see our students, to see the world around us, to see the authors we are reading, and to see our various subjects of study, whether we are training to become discipline-specific teachers or generalists. Here, we take up the word "seeing" as it relates to the heart of philosophic gazing or contemplation (*theoria*), and we practice seeing and learning about seeing by experimenting with teaching as a way of life. Put another way, and in terms often used generically in B. Ed. programs, we are concerned, on the one hand, with learners and learning (i.e., with learning to see our students, and with teaching our students to see as well), and, on the other hand, with teachers and teaching. From a logistical viewpoint, when designing a philosophy of education course for a B.Ed. program, it is important to make it fit within broad, accepted categories. Divisions such as teachers and teaching, and learners and learning are flexible, and can be approached philosophically in a hands-on, practical way; work within such a course might even be embedded in learning tasks that concern curriculum design and practice.

Once one has found a way to situate philosophy of education within the over-arching framework of a B.Ed. program, the next step is to consider how to create "authentic" learning experiences for students that invite them to partake in the spirit of philosophy. The program of work I have developed for B. Ed. courses requires good daily, experimental efforts from students that they must document in open journal format. I recommend journaling over any other form of writing, since journaling is perhaps the most authentic form of writing. According to assessment experts Newmann, Marks, and Gamoran (1996), authenticity in task design requires three central components: construction of knowledge, disciplined inquiry, and value beyond school. Philosophy-driven writing in open journal format satisfies all three requirements because it beckons students not simply to absorb inert facts and information but to comprehend, apply, analyze, synthesize, and evaluate what they are learning through experimentation with a wide variety of processes and products in which there is no onus toward predetermined benchmarks for success, but only toward openness and receptivity. Moreover, the journal format not only facilitates the so-called construction of learning; it inspires disciplined inquiry, and in particular, deep self-inquiry. The writing students do for these journal assignments, in my experience, can be full of passion and interest that takes them in all kinds of previously unexplored directions. Reflecting in journals allows students the freedom to wonder, to contemplate their experiences, and to generate insights. Finally, open journal writing in philosophy of education most especially has value beyond school (Newmann et al., 1996). Indeed, many of my B.Ed. students have told me that our courses together had less to do with the nuts and bolts of teaching processes and far more to do with building awareness and resonance with the transformational properties of education.

Student work in these philosophy of education courses gravitates around the independent as well as cooperative/conversational exploration of foundational education philosophy texts. Students read and think about these discourses, of course, but they are especially asked to experiment with or live these texts during the semester, journaling their findings as they proceed. Ordinarily, I supply students with a long, non-exhaustive list of writing topics that may serve as helpful prompts for those who require assistance getting started with their journal writing. This is an important consideration, since many students have never encountered such an open form of writing in a post-secondary setting, and its novelty may cause anxiety for some.

Hadot's (1995) insights about philosophy as a way of life show us that it is important to design topic and writing prompts to ensure that students are grappling not only with a variety of philosophical discourses, but also that they are experimenting with a number of different spiritual exercises related to these discourses, and that they are writing about their encounters with each in turn. Remember: although in a B.Ed. program, we cannot shirk our responsibility to teach to the acquisition of career competencies for the purpose of professional accreditation and certification, the underlying, authentic purpose of philosophy of education is to involve ourselves experimentally and on a daily basis in both the active and contemplative aspects of wisdom-seeking. Being two-fold by nature, philosophic practices are well-suited to help B. Ed. students take up teaching as this self-same, two-fold way of life involving contemplative, as well as active wisdom-seeking, rather than simply as a job or career choice.

Journaling their experimental findings in relation to a broad range of philosophic discourses and spiritual exercises holds much potential as a reflective and metacognitive activity. Students constantly assess themselves in such self-selected tasks. However, it is noteworthy that in the competency movement, the idea that students might assess themselves regarding their core competencies is discredited. As Drisko writes,

> Persons of established competency, or measures they create, must assess learner competencies. The learner alone cannot assess competence. Assessment of competence presupposes the evaluator is qualified: possesses the knowledge, values, and skills being examined and has considerable experience in their application. This assumption is common in the academy and in business and industry. (2014, p. 420)

Likewise, instructor-led assessment practices generally play an important role in philosophy of education design. Nevertheless, it seems equally true that self-assessment remains an important aspect not only of learning but also of developing career competencies. Hence, in my own philosophy of education designs, although I am involved in the journal assessment process, student self-assessment is assigned a central role in all their learning tasks. In particular, I use student self-assessment practices to guide me as their instructor. Students themselves direct me toward matters of most interest, experimental episodes most puzzling, enjoyable, or troublesome for them; these self-assessments are also as a means for students to indicate where they felt their learning to have been most significant or relevant in relation to the different imposed competency criteria that underlie all B.Ed. programming.

As an accompaniment to the journaling prompts provided for experimentation with philosophic discourses and spiritual exercises, I equip students with a set of black-line masters for a cue card self-evaluation system that encourages them to become partners in assessment during their studies in philosophy of education (see Figure 4.1).

I have adapted this middle/high school cue card self-assessment strategy from the portfolio system developed by Anne Davies and associates (2000). As a part of my philosophy of education course designs, in addition to daily philosophic experimentation and journaling, student-teachers are asked periodically to review their journal writing entries and select representative contributions for each cue card item. They will then photocopy the pertinent cue card from the course syllabus. Having responded briefly to each cue card prompt, they next cut out and affix these cards within their own hard-copy journals. Figure 4.1 only showcases a small few of the rich self-assessments associated with the open, experimental journal format; in practice, a much broader range of assessment criteria should use many more cue card prompts for students to consider.

By handing over some power or authority to my students, and by drawing them into decision-making around the formative and summative assessment of their KSAs as teachers-in-training, I find that they are more readily weaned away from educationally-debilitating fixations upon marks and from

DESIGNING TEACHER EDUCATION 109

FIGURE 4.1   Some sample cue card self-assessment tools, including ones based upon identification of core B. Ed. program competencies

supposing there is only one way to think about or evaluate what they have done in school: namely, the grade. Indeed, one of the great virtues of Davies' portfolio cue card system (as I have adapted it here to philosophic journal writing) is that it bids students leave behind such grading fixations, in part by showing them how there are many more rich, thoughtful ways of evaluating and assessing their work than a reductionistic concern with outcomes and marks. By reducing student-teacher concerns with such ego-centered, petty things, Davies' approach can be harnessed to help student-teachers enter into the experimental spirit of philosophy and of teaching as a way of life. Putting aside lesser goods in pursuit of the *summum bonum*, they are better enabled to seek the truth about being itself (the contemplative aspect of teaching) and likewise entice others toward this self-same pursuit of the truth about what is (the active aspect of teaching).

Two caveats need to be considered when applying Davies' system within a formal B.Ed. program. First, let me reiterate that many of the self-assessment cue cards I have incorporated into my philosophy of education course designs are taken directly from Davies' widely accepted work. However, it is important to note that Davies' junior/senior high school self-assessment system fails to address either the official list of KSA outcomes associated with requirements for teacher certification skills or the core competencies that must underlie B. Ed. programming. Therefore, in addition to using Davies' self-assessment criteria, I have opted to include other cards that focus on the ten competencies of the B.Ed. program in the university where I have most recently been employed (see the sample cards in left-hand column of Figure 4.1). Obviously, other B. Ed. programs might have different lists of such competencies, based upon government-mandated benchmarks related to acquiring KSAs deemed essential to competent teaching practices in different jurisdictions. Philosophy of education instructors will need to tweak these competency cue cards to suit local expectations for teacher certification.

Second, although Davies' cue card system has great value for application in a philosophy of education course, it cannot be a stand-alone measure. In alignment with Drisko's (2014) observation about the need for expert assessment in relation to core competencies, I have always ensured that the rich and diverse cue card self-assessments used in my philosophy of education courses are scrutinized by an expert using an instructor-scored rubric with core career competencies listed as its underlying framework (see Figure 4.2).

Student Journal (Teacher-Assessed Component)

Competency	Description
1	Journal demonstrates evidence that student is seeking/developing ways to build affirmative relationships with children.
2	Journal demonstrates evidence that student is seeking/developing ways to apply theories of curriculum, learning, and assessment to the development of programs.
3	Journal demonstrates evidence that student is seeking/developing ways to build learning communities.
4	Journal demonstrates evidence that student is seeking/developing ways to design teaching and learning scenarios that include inquiry-based learning.
5	Journal demonstrates evidence that student is seeking/developing ways to design inclusive learning experiences that recognize and accommodate all children, including those with exceptional learning needs.
6	Journal demonstrates evidence that student is seeking/developing ways to engage in shared praxis.
7	Journal demonstrates evidence that student is seeking/developing ways to design and implement programs that incorporate attention to cultural realities and diversities.
8	Journal demonstrates evidence that student is seeking/developing ways to understand critical and creative thinking as essential to learning in all programs.
9	Journal demonstrates evidence that student is seeking/developing ways to demonstrate the essential dispositions that characterize a professional educator from the Education Program.
10	Journal demonstrates evidence that student is seeking/developing ways to address non-academic barriers to learning by applying a variety of management strategies and effective classroom techniques.
Student Self Assessment Component	Student's meta-cognitive commentary on required/specified selections from the Journal demonstrates that he/she has been sufficiently thorough, honest, and reflective in his/her developing understanding of teaching and in the demonstration of teacher competencies.
Completeness	Student demonstrated evidence of daily journaling practices as stipulated in the course outline.

Grading Key
E = Excellent
Pf = Proficient
S = Satisfactory
L = Limited
P = Poor

FIGURE 4.2 Sample instructor-scored competencies rubric for third way philosophy of education design

Conclusion

Great care has been taken in the design and delivery of this third way of bringing the study of the philosophy of education to preservice students so that they will be exposed to good, authentic tasks for experimentation with the pursuit of wisdom that they might likewise be enticed toward practicing teaching not simply as their chosen career, but as a way of life. The essential challenge of any philosophy of education course that adopts this third approach is that, although in its instructional design it must always pay careful homage to the mandated, hegemonic demands for demonstration of career competencies, in its heart-of-hearts, it always teaches past these petty things. Good education—even in a professional teacher training program—should always in some fashion follow Christ's command to "Render therefore unto Caesar the things which be Caesar's, and unto God the things which be God's" (Luke 20:25). In a very real sense, any genuine learning about teaching as a way of life in pursuit of wisdom happens in spite of the ordinary focus in B.Ed. programs on core competencies and not because of their successful achievement and demonstration. Nonetheless, the cultivation of these higher philosophical concerns about wisdom within a B.Ed. program is not wholly out of place. To use a crude allegory, just as the Buddhist monk comes to understand the Middle Way through practicing emptiness in his daily chores of hauling wood, washing floors, and fetching water, so too might the student-teacher learn the teacher's way of life by performing his or her teacherly duties in the proper spirit.

This matter of spirit is key. No amount of competency demonstration is worth much unless attention to the two-fold spirit of the teacher lies somewhere at its foundation. While teaching as a way of life is a core value as described here, it awkwardly problematizes all striving toward assessments which we seek to employ in this third way of approaching philosophy of education.

References

Aquinas, S. T. (1966). *Summa Theologica* (Vol. 46, J. Aumann, Trans.). London: Blackfriars. Aquinas (2a2ae.179–182).

Aristotle. (2001). *The basic works* (R. McKeon, Ed.). New York, NY: Modern Library.

Baughman, J. A., Brumm, T. J., & Mickelson, S. K. (2012). Student professional development: Competency-based learning and assessment. *Journal of Technology Studies, 38*(2), 115–127.

Bransford, J., Brown, A. L., & Cocking, R. R. (2000). *How people learn: Brain, mind, experience, and school.* Washington, DC: National Academic Press.

Burgoyne, J. G. (1993). The competence movement: Issues, stakeholders and prospects. *Personnel Review, 22*(6), 6–13.

Drisko, J. W. (2014). Competencies and their assessment. *Journal of Social Work Education, 50*, 414–426.

Gardner, S. K. (2009). Student development theory: A primer. *ASHE Higher Education Report, 34*(6), 15–28.

Government of Alberta. (1997). *Teaching quality standard applicable to the provision of basic education in Alberta* (Ministerial Order #016/97). Edmonton: Government of Alberta.

Government of Alberta. (2016). *Department of education draft teaching quality standard.* Teaching and Leadership Excellence: Alberta Education.

Government of Alberta. (2018). *Teaching quality standard.* Alberta Education. Retrieved from https://education.alberta.ca/media/3739620/standardsdoc-tqs-_fa-web-2018-01-17.pdf

Gregory, K., Cameron, C., & Davies, A. (2000). *Self-assessment and goal-setting.* Courtenay: Building Connections Publishing.

Hadot, P. (1995). *Philosophy as a way of life* (A. I. Davidson, Ed., M. Chase, Trans.). Oxford: Blackwell Publishing.

Hadot, P. (2002). *What is ancient philosophy?* (M. Chase, Trans.). London: Harvard University Press.

Hoffmann, T. (1999). The meanings of competency. *Journal of European Industrial Training, 23*(6), 275–285.

Jones, E. A., & Voorhees, R. A. (2002). *Defining and assessing learning: Exploring competency-based initiatives.* Report of the National Post-secondary Education Cooperative Working Group on Competency-Based Initiatives in Post-secondary Education. Retrieved from http://nces.ed.gov/pubs2002/2002159.pdf

Kingsley, P. (1995). *Ancient philosophy, mystery, and magic: Empedocles and Pythagorean tradition.* Oxford: Clarendon Press.

Kingsley, P. (1999). *In the dark places of wisdom.* Point Reyes: The Golden Sufi Centre.

Kingsley, P. (2003). *Reality.* Point Reyes: The Golden Sufi Centre.

Newmann, F. M., Marks, H. M., & Gamoran, A. (1996). Authentic pedagogy and student performance. *American Journal of Education, 104*(4), 280–312.

Pieper, J. (1992). *In defense of philosophy* (L. Krauth, Trans.). San Francisco, CA: Ignatius Press.

Pieper, J. (1998). *Happiness and contemplation* (Richard & C. Winston, Trans.). South Bend: St. Augustine's Press.

Pieper, J. (2004). *For the love of wisdom: Essays on the nature of philosophy* (B. Wald, Ed., R. Wasserman, Trans.). San Francisco, CA: Ignatius Press.

Uzdavinys, A. (2004). *The golden chain: An anthology of Pythagorean and Platonic philosophy.* Bloomington: World Wisdom.

Uzdavinys, A. (2008). *Philosophy as a rite of rebirth: From ancient Egypt to Neoplatonism.* Westbury: The Prometheus Trust.

Uzdavinys, A. (2011). *Orpheus and the roots of Neoplatonism.* London: The Matheson Trust.

Woodruffe, C. (1993). What is meant by a competency? *Leadership & Organization Development Journal, 14*(1), 29–36.

CHAPTER 5

Looking Forward

Cecille DePass and Kim Koh

To encourage critical thinking and productive discourse in the theory and practice of assessment literacy, our book concludes with a problem scenario accompanied with some key questions to guide discussion and future actions, as well as some recommendations for designing assessment curriculum and authentic learning tasks to enhance the quality of teaching and learning in teacher preparation programs.[1]

Fostering Exemplary Assessment Practices: A Problem Scenario[2]

Having successfully completed her first degree in the humanities, with a 3.9 CGPA, Mary Lu, a preservice teacher or student teacher is enrolled in a teacher preparation program at a western Canadian university. Mary Lu has always been determined to pursue a teaching career. Toward the end of her final semester in the two-year teacher preparation program, Mary is busy completing her last three major assignments in three courses. She has found that the most difficult task is to write a research paper, worth 40% of her final grade in one of the required courses. Over the past three semesters, almost all her assignments involved group work and presentations. In one of the theory courses, she did well on class quizzes and the final exam, and what she needed to do was to digest the lecture notes and textbook information. The quizzes and final exam consisted of multiple-choice and short-answer items.

Since the first semester of enrolling in the teacher preparation program, Mary has continuously challenged herself to excel in all course requirements including the rigorous and often exhausting practicums in her assigned schools. For the final research paper, she is determined to produce exemplary work so she can maintain a high GPA. During her educational studies, she has been actively involved as a volunteer and leader of the faculty's Education Students' Association and, off-campus, has led the Big Sisters' program. She has aspired to and is determined to obtain all A+ or A grades so she will be on the Dean's Honors List when she graduates in spring. In this last semester of her program, she has begun to apply for a teaching job. She hopes to receive an interview and a full-time job offer from one of the major school jurisdictions by the end of spring.

Prior to writing her research paper, Mary framed her questions and submitted her proposal to her course instructor, Dr. Tom Braveheart. The proposal was reviewed and approved by Dr. Braveheart. Mary found a couple of written comments on her proposal: "You are on the right track" and "Good Job!" Currently, Mary is completing her writing of the research paper. She sits at her laptop to review her research notes which include information from an extensive literature review and as important, astute observations from her case/log book compiled during her lengthy practicum/field experience. She begins a meticulous review of her information. However, Mary is so exhausted that she falls into a deep sleep. She dreams so vividly that it appears as if she is living each dream.[3]

Dream 1. Mary is suddenly aware of standing in a banquet hall at a massive, five star, all-inclusive resort in China, at which the tables in the dining center are laden with dishes of delicious food. Everything in the room appears perfect, from elaborate décor to furniture and from table and place settings to the gourmet banquet. The Chinese food has obviously been produced by master chefs. In her dream, she savors the delicious smells and imagines she can taste the food. However, as she looks at the diners sitting at the round tables, she sees that each diner holds chopsticks at least three feet long. Accordingly, it is impossible for each person to use the chopsticks to feed himself/herself. She is shocked and quite distressed.

Dream 2. Still asleep, she goes into a new dream. She is in another banquet hall. Everything appears to be exactly the same as in the first dream. However, in this dining center, Mary observes that the diners are happy. They are chatting, laughing, and sharing stories. She sees too, that the diners are well fed and content. As she looks more closely at the diners, she notes that unlike the first dream, in the second dream, the diners are feeding each other with the three-foot-long chopsticks. None of the diners attempts to feed himself/herself. Mary wakes up. Her mind is absolutely clear. She is no longer exhausted and overwhelmed by the demands of her final research paper. Mary decides to speak with Dr. Braveheart as soon as, possible. She plans to ask him to encourage the students to contribute meaningful input in the conceptualization of the final paper's assessment criteria and its written standards.

Prior to her meeting, what questions should Mary prepare to ask Dr. Braveheart to ensure that each preservice teacher in the course will appreciate the final paper's significance and produce the best paper possible?

Guiding questions for discussion:
1. Why is the final paper weighted at 40%?
2. Throughout the semester, how do the preservice teachers know, in observable terms, that they are making progress toward achieving their individual learning goals?
3. In what ways will the instructor and preservice teachers use the written assessment information?
4. Does attaining a high grade for the final paper really matter? Explain whether, to what extent, and in what ways it might or might not be important.
5. In what ways does completing the final paper prepare the preservice teachers for their future teaching careers?
6. What are the explicit criteria and standards used to assess the quality/merit of the final paper?
7. Explain whether and why formative assessment will be incorporated in any way and at any time, into the process of completing the final paper.
8. Will the preservice teachers be given opportunities to negotiate and provide appropriate inputs in developing criteria and standards to be adopted in the final scoring rubric?
9. Will the preservice teachers be allowed, in small groups: (i) To brainstorm ideas for the assessment with their peers? (ii) To provide peer feedback on the draft papers prior to preparing and submitting the final papers for summative evaluation by the instructor?
10. Based on your reading of the book's chapters, are there other key issues you think Mary Lu should discuss with Dr. Braveheart? If so, identify at least three issues.
11. For future consideration: With the instructor's approval, and working with a small group, identify key assessment issues and organize for your class a panel that includes some authorities who design quality assessment for learning and teaching in: (i) an elementary or secondary/high school in your school board/district; (ii) the provincial or state government. Include in the panel government policymakers and officers, and any other stakeholders who play significant policy development and assessment roles.

Designing Assessment Curriculum and Authentic Learning Tasks for Quality Teaching and Learning in Teacher Preparation Programs

The problem scenario aims to generate thoughts on the design of high-quality assessment tasks to enhance the learning experiences of preservice teachers or student teachers. We believe that the problem scenario can also be modified and expanded to meet the needs of inservice teacher professional development in educational assessment (i.e., workshops and courses) and in other disciplines.

In the design and development of an assessment course for preservice teachers in a teacher preparation program, the first author of this book has adopted PBL, which is one of the signature pedagogies (with case-based learning and place-based learning approaches). PBL has been incorporated into the program to improve the quality of teaching and learning of the student teachers. As a learner- or student-centered pedagogical approach, PBL utilizes a problem scenario to initiate, focus, and motivate student learning. The problem is complex and rooted in the real-world context of the learners. Additionally, the problem must be current and reflect a typical problem encountered by professionals in the field. For example, a teacher must understand the theory and practice of assessment for learning in view of the global education reform movement. The instructor in a PBL lesson plays a pivotal role as a facilitator of learning rather than being a teacher-expert. Students working in small groups are actively engaged in defining the problem, identifying learning goals, researching and collecting relevant information from different sources, brainstorming possible solutions, and finally, mapping and setting out an action plan (Koh, 2014; Koh & Tan, 2016). More important, students engage in self-directed learning (e.g., searching for additional relevant resources) outside the classroom (Barrows & Tamblyn, 1980). Hence, PBL is deemed to develop student teachers' higher-order competencies such as critical thinking, complex problem-solving, communication, collaboration, and self-directed learning.

Lee Shulman (2005) defines signature pedagogies as "the types of teaching that organize the fundamental ways in which future practitioners are educated for their new professions" (p. 52). Novices are often instructed in critical aspects of the three fundamental dimensions of professional work – to think, perform, and act with integrity. This suggests that student teachers and new teachers need to learn how to think and act like teachers (Darling-Hammond, 2006). Similar to Shulman (2005) and Darling-Hammond (2006), Sawyer (2008) has called for teachers to become knowledge workers, with equivalent skills to other professional knowledge workers such as lawyers, doctors, nurses, and engineers. It is important that teachers deeply understand the theoretical principles and the latest knowledge about how children learn. Additionally, teachers need to become conversant with the authentic practices of highly trained scientists, historians, mathematics, and/or literary critics. Such arguments indicate the merit of "using authentic assessments of teaching—cases, exhibitions, portfolios, and problem-based inquiries (or action research)—as tools to support teacher learning" in teacher preparation programs (Darling-Hammond &

Snyder, 2000, p. 523). Authentic assessments of teaching align with Wiggins's (1989) authentic assessment, which advocates K–12 students' engagement in solving real-world problems that are typically encountered by experts or professionals in the field (Koh, 2017). Authentic assessments with student teachers and new teachers will prepare them to adopt and use similar assessment methods with students when they begin teaching in K–12 schools. In short, it is essential for teacher educators to model exemplary instructional and assessment practices to student teachers in their courses.

Responses to Dream 1

Dream 1 reflects Mary Lu's anxiety over the negative consequences of conventional assessments. It demonstrates the ugly side of using assessment for summative purposes. The research paper counts for 40% toward the final grade. If Dr. Braveheart intends to use it as a summative assessment of how much and/or how well student teachers have learned from his course, it could have detrimental effects on student teachers' learning and motivation. Many might have shared Mary's dream. The use of the research paper as a summative assessment will preclude effective formative assessment or assessment for learning practices by both the instructor and students. As a result, student teachers are likely to focus more on the final product, at the expense of the process of writing and revising their research papers. It will reinforce a performance mindset. Student teachers become more competitive and self-centered if attaining an A+ or A grade is their only goal. It may also defeat the purpose and limit the potential of the research paper as an authentic assessment in which student teachers are given the opportunity to learn to use research evidence to support their classroom practices. Evidence-based or research-informed practice has become one of the requirements for teaching in 21st-century classrooms. As such, teacher preparation programs around the globe create ample opportunities for preservice teachers to make meaningful connections between research and practice. Teacher educators are urged to not only share research-based practice with student teachers but also to actively pursue recent scholarship in teaching and learning.

As for the course instructor, using a rubric (if any) will not add value to his feedback practice if the sole purpose of using the research paper is to fulfill accountability demands, that is, by assigning the grades. Other concerns include: To what extent are the student teachers involved in the negotiation of the assessment criteria and standards for judging their research papers? How do the criteria and standards align with the learning objectives identified in the course outline? If Dr. Braveheart did not address these concerns, it means he might have failed to model exemplary assessment practices to the student teachers. Finally, at the program level, what does it mean if a student teacher scores an A+ in Dr. Braveheart's course? Will it indicate that the student teacher meets the professional teaching standards established by the province or state?

Responses to Dream 2

Dream 2 serves as a contrast to Dream 1. It reflects the hope arising from the positive effects of authentic assessment. Properly designed, authentic assessments provide many opportunities for students to actively engage in learning and conducting authentic intellectual work (Koh, 2017). Authentic assessments allow students to demonstrate what they know and can do with their knowledge and skills. This represents the good side of assessment. As such, Mary is no longer worried about the demands of writing a research paper. Her focus should be on learning and how to take responsibility for her own learning throughout the process. She would begin to value the research paper as an authentic assessment in which she could use relevant literature and research evidence to argue for her practices. She also knows the importance of evidence-based practice or research-informed practice. This helps her think and act like a teacher. Further, as Koh points out in the first chapter of this book, shifting from a performance mindset to a growth mindset will enable Mary to engage in self-directed and lifelong learning. Mary will then take the initiative to approach her instructor, Dr. Braveheart, and lead the discussion on the assessment criteria, standards, and weighting of the research paper. Once Dr. Braveheart clarifies all these components, Mary plans to engage in self-assessment by checking her research paper against the rubric which will be developed by the instructor and students. She will also invite one of her coursemates to exchange their draft papers for peer feedback (i.e., peer assessment). More important, Mary realizes that a strong academic record is important, but it is not the only indicator or source of evidence of success in the teacher preparation program. Other indicators or sources of evidence include her active participation in the Education Students' Association and other co-curricular activities, her presentations at several conferences, and her mentoring of a student with special needs in the off-campus Big Sisters program (i.e., community engagement). Her exemplary teaching performance, lesson planning, and collaboration with other teachers during practicums has yielded a strong reference letter from her partner or associate teacher. Last summer, she worked as an undergraduate intern in a research project on developing preservice teachers' assessment literacy. This provides her with a second reference letter from the project's Principal Investigator who is able to speak about Mary's strengths and potential contributions to evidence-based teaching. Finally, her success of being hired as a full-time teacher depends on how well she presents herself during the face-to-face teaching job interview. Such an interview draws heavily on her critical and reflective thinking, and interpersonal communications skills.

In Dream 2, Dr. Braveheart's intention may be to use the research paper as an authentic assessment which helps promote student teachers' critical and reflective thinking about evidence-based practice. His instructional plans can incorporate formative assessment, such as student self-assessment and peer feedback in the learning process. Although his written comments on Mary's research proposal are brief and less informative, he is willing to spend more time with her to provide oral feedback. Therefore, he is happy that Mary Lu and her coursemates take the initiative to ask questions and negotiate the assessment criteria and standards with him. These learner attributes fall within the notion of assessment for learning. Dr. Braveheart's conceptions of assessment might have been influenced by his previous educational experiences, sociocultural background, and institutional constraints. He knows the importance of improving his written feedback on students' assignments, despite the academic challenges he encounters.

Conclusion

In this chapter, we present a problem scenario along with some guiding questions, as well as the importance of designing high-quality assessment to support teaching and learning in teacher preparation programs. We also provide our responses to the two different dreams embedded within the problem scenario based on two different approaches to assessment: conventional assessment versus authentic assessment (Koh & Luke, 2009). Teaching and assessment in today's K–12 schools and higher education institutions, including teacher preparation programs, have become more complex than ever. What is essential for us is to enrich preservice and inservice teachers' professional learning opportunities by taking into account the following acts:

> their thinking and actions in situations that are experience based and problem-oriented and that include or simulate actual acts of teaching. Such acts of teaching include plans for and reflections on teaching and learning, as well as activities featuring direct interactions with students. (Darling-Hammond & Snyder, 2000, p. 524)

Such a view reiterates the importance of experiential learning and learning by doing as advocated by John Dewey (1938), in his groundbreaking book, *Experience and Education*. Finally, our book includes the authors' reflections of being students and later, teacher educators in their respective sociocultural and geopolitical contexts. Although the authors' views and experiences differ, they complement each other in their discourse on an important topic: developing teachers' assessment literacy.

There is an urgent need for teacher preparation and professional development programs to "equip teachers with contemporary knowledge about learning and assessment, especially the knowledge needed to develop tasks that would elicit students' thinking skills or make it possible to assess their growth and progress toward competence" (Pellegrino, Chudowsky, & Glaser, 2001). Pellegrino (2014) further emphasizes that "preservice teacher education and continuing professional development are needed to help teachers formulate models of learning progression so they can identify students' naïve or initial sense-making strategies and build on those to move students toward more sophisticated understandings" (p. 242). Taken together, these underscore the importance of building teachers' capacity in the design and use of authentic assessment to support student learning. Teachers' use of well-developed authentic tasks and rubrics that capture learning progression will enable them to develop diagnostic competence, which is an essential element of formative assessment or assessment for learning. Over the past decade, several assessment innovations include the Educational Testing Service's Cognitively Based Assessment of, for, and as Learning (CBAL, Bennett, 2010) Initiative and the use of evidence-centered assessment design (ECD) to develop game-based assessments (Shutes & Torres, 2012). ECD helps instructional designers take advantage of developments from measurement, assessment, technology, cognitive psychology, and learning sciences (Mislevy & Haertel, 2006) and it ensures that the assessment of students' knowledge, skills, and attributes (KSAs) is supported by evidentiary arguments. Such an important form of validity is only tenable when "assessments are grounded in empirical evidence of cognition and learning" (Pellegrino, 2014, p. 239). In short, these initiatives need to reach beyond test developers, psychometricians, and educational researchers. More important, if we envision students to be exposed to high-quality assessments, teachers need support to develop their "designers' eyes" in educational assessment.

Notes

1 Both authors contributed equally to this chapter. DePass wrote the problem scenario and Koh provided the solutions.

2 The problem scenario is based on observations and reflections concerning ways in which the more cue-conscious and cue-assertive preservice teachers tackle their final exit papers in the B. Ed. program in which the three authors have taught. None of the preservice teachers suggested, either orally or in writing, that they should have meaningful input to the development of the final assessment criteria used in the undergraduate teacher preparation program. Admittedly, there was considerable and ongoing discussion between the instructors concerning the instructors' expectations and the merit and value of the final written papers.

3 The dream sequences are adapted from a well-known fable, "Heaven and Hell," with origins attributed to China, the Middle East, and parts of Europe. This version is highly modified, but the core concepts remain the same. For further information, please read MacDonald (1992). Also see several versions online.

References

Barrows, H., & Tamblyn, R. (1980). *Problem-based learning: An approach to medical education*. New York, NY: Springer.

Bennett, R. E. (2010). Cognitively Based Assessment of, for, and as Learning (CBAL): A preliminary theory of action for summative and formative assessment. *Measurement, 8*(2–3), 70–91.

Darling-Hammond, L. (2006). Constructing 21st-century teacher education. *Journal of Teacher Education, 57*(X), 1–15.

Darling-Hammond, L., & Snyder, J. (2000). Authentic assessment of teaching in context. *Teaching and Teacher Education, 16*(5–6), 523–545.

Dewey, J. (1938). *Experience and education*. New York, NY: Collier Books.

Koh, K. (2014). Developing preservice teachers' assessment literacy: A problem-based learning approach. In P. Preciado Babb (Ed.), *Proceedings of the IDEAS rising to the challenge* (pp. 113–120). Calgary: Werklund School of Education, University of Calgary.

Koh, K. (2017). Authentic assessment. In G. Noblit (Ed.), *Oxford research encyclopedia of education*. doi:10.1093/acrefore/9780190264093.013.22

Koh, K., & Luke, A. (2009). Authentic and conventional assessment in Singapore schools: An empirical study of teacher assignments and student work. *Assessment in Education: Principles, Policy & Practice, 16*(3), 291–318.

Koh, K., & Tan, C. (2016). Promoting reflection in pre-service teachers through problem-based learning: An example from Canada. *Reflective Practice, 17*(3), 347–356.

MacDonald, M. (1992). Heaven and hell. In *Peace tales: World folktales to talk about*. Hamden, CT: Linnet Books.

Mislevy, R. J., & Haertel, G. D. (2006). Implications of evidence-centered design for educational testing. *Educational Measurement: Issues and Practice, 25*(4), 6–20.

Pellegrino, J. W. (2014). A learning sciences perspective on the design and use of assessment in education. In R. K. Sawyer (Ed.), *The Cambridge handbook of the learning sciences* (2nd ed., pp. 233–252). New York, NY: Cambridge University Press.

Pellegrino, J. W., Chudowsky, N., & Glaser, R. (2001). *Knowing what students know: The science and design of educational assessment.* Washington, DC: National Academic Press.

Sawyer, R. K. (2008). *Optimizing learning: Implications of learning sciences research.* CERI/ OECD International Conference "Learning in the 21st Century: Research, Innovation and Policy. Retrieved from http://www.oecd.org/dataoecd/39/52/40554221.pdf

Shulman, L. S. (2005). Signature pedagogies in the professions. *Daedalus, 134*(3), 52–59.

Shute, V. J., & Torres, R. (2012). Where streams converge: Using evidence centered design to assess quest to learn. In M. C. Mayrath, J. Clarke-Midura, & D. H. Robinson (Eds.), *Technology-based assessments for 21st century skills: Theoretical and practical implications from modern research* (pp. 91–124). Charlotte, NC: Information Age.

Wiggins, G. (1989). A true test: Toward more authentic and equitable assessment. *Phi Delta Kappan, 70,* 703–713.

Index

21st-century competencies or capabilities 1, 2, 12, 19, 23, 59, 60, 64, 66–68, 70, 71, 74, 81, 88, 89
21st-century skills 10, 78

academic and non-academic skills 10, 15, 67, 73
academic credentials 46–48
academic skills 15, 69, 73
accountability 8, 10, 12, 16, 17, 21, 41, 64, 68, 69, 101, 104, 118
action plan 117
active participation 73, 119
acts of teaching 88, 120
Adamson 60
Adie, L. 2, 19
affirmation action policy 9
Alberta Assessment Consortium (AAC) 86
Alberta education 67, 70, 71
Alberta government 61, 67, 71, 99
Alberta Initiative for School Improvement (AISI) 70, 71, 90
Alberta, Canada 4, 60–62, 76, 99
alternative forms of assessment 1, 10, 12, 15, 20, 59, 60, 68, 73, 82
American Educational Research Association (AERA) 16, 17, 69, 72
Aquinas, Thomas 104
Aristotle 103, 104
Ash, A. 34, 38
assessment as learning 16, 20, 76
assessment capacity 2
assessment courses 3, 75–89, 117
assessment criteria 11, 54, 108, 110, 115, 118–120, 122
assessment curricula 1
assessment curriculum and resources 23, 86, 88
assessment data 16, 21, 62, 75, 79
assessment for accountability 17, 69
assessment for learning 1, 12, 15–17, 20, 21, 36, 59, 68, 70, 71, 78, 83–86, 88–90, 117, 118, 120, 121
assessment knowledge and skills 1, 17, 21, 89

assessment literacy or competence 1–5, 7, 14–23, 59–61, 75, 87–91, 114, 120, 121
assessment methods 2, 12, 15, 18, 19, 22, 48, 59, 75, 78, 87–89, 112
assessment of learning 4, 16, 20, 21, 73, 75, 76, 84, 88
assessment practice 1, 2, 11, 14–16, 18–22, 51, 60, 68, 70, 73, 75–78, 82, 85, 86, 88, 90, 91, 108, 114, 118, 119
assessment tools 82, 84, 106, 109
Australia 19
authentic assessment tasks 23, 69, 84
authentic assessment 2, 12–14, 18, 21, 23, 36, 59, 69–71, 76, 77, 81, 83, 84, 88–90, 117–121
authentic intellectual work 13, 69, 119
authentic learning experiences 72, 106
authentic learning tasks 114, 116–118
authenticity 106

balanced assessment systems 16
banausic demands 104
Barbados 39
B.Ed. program 76, 82, 98, 100, 101, 105–111
behaviorist learning approach 9, 11, 14
behaviorist view of learning 12
beliefs 10, 13, 14, 20, 27, 59, 68, 88–90
Bennett, R. E. 41
Bernstein's framing and classification 20
Black, P. 17, 70
Brookhart, S. 17
Brown, G. 40
business and industry 101, 108

Cambridge Assessment International (formerly, Cambridge International Examinations) 39–41, 44, 63, 64
Canada 3, 4, 7, 8, 11, 19, 22, 27, 28, 34, 44–51, 55, 60–62, 65, 66, 76, 86, 89, 98, 99
Canadian universities 3, 33, 35, 88, 114
Caribbean Examination Council (CXC) 41
Caribbean 3, 28, 37, 38, 40–44, 54
Cazden, C. 20
Chapman, O. 89
character and citizenship 73

China 4, 7, 32–36, 38, 51, 115, 122
Clarke, Austin 39, 40, 43, 44
classroom assessment 1, 2, 8, 9, 15–17, 59, 60, 69, 75, 77, 82, 86, 90
classroom discourse 11, 20
Clinton, Hilary Rodham 52
cognitive psychology 121
Cognitively Based Assessment of, for, and as Learning (CBAL) 121
collaboration 1, 10, 12, 22, 53, 60, 66, 67, 81, 88, 117, 119
colonial education 37, 39–41
communication 1, 10, 12, 22, 32, 36, 42, 52, 60, 66, 67, 69, 71, 81, 88, 117, 120
competencies 1, 2, 4, 10, 12, 15–17, 19, 21–23, 59, 60, 64, 66–68, 70, 71, 73, 74, 75, 78, 80, 81, 87–89, 91, 97–111, 117, 121
competency-based education 97–111, 121
complex problem-solving 1, 10, 12, 22, 60, 66, 69, 81, 88, 117
conceptions of assessment 3, 7, 11, 14, 81, 88–90, 120
construction of knowledge 106
context-dependent 19, 21
conventional assessment 20, 72, 73, 90, 118, 120
CORE program 72
core subjects 62, 66, 68, 71, 75
core values 27, 67, 111
course design 97, 98, 101, 108, 109
creativity and innovation 10, 22, 60, 66, 67
criteria and standards 11, 116, 118, 120
critical inquiry 11, 20
critical thinking 1, 4, 10, 12, 22, 31, 66, 67, 69, 88, 104, 114, 117
cross-curricular competencies 59, 67, 75
cue aggressive learners 33
cue assertive learners 29, 32, 33, 37, 51
cue card self-assessment tools 108–110
cue conscious learners 32
cue deaf learners 33, 37
cultural contexts 3, 90
curricular goals 2
curriculum design or redesign 59, 60, 66–68, 71, 98, 106

Darling-Hammond, L. 60, 88, 117
Davies, A. 108

Davis, B. 90
Deep understanding 69, 76, 84
DeLuca, C. 22
DePass' experiences with summative examinations 32, 118
design, selection, and use of authentic assessments 2, 59
developing teachers' assessment literacy 1–5, 7, 14, 22, 23, 60, 75, 87, 90, 91, 121
Dewey, J. 34, 121
diagnostic competence 121
disciplinary knowledge 89
disciplined inquiry 69, 70, 106, 107
discourses 4, 10, 11, 19–21, 76, 85, 103, 107, 108, 114, 121
dispositions 19, 69, 73, 87, 91
Dolakia, Jagruti 28, 53
dream 29, 53, 115, 118–120, 122
Drisko, J. W. 107, 110
Dweck, C. 10
dynamic social practice 19, 21

Earl, L. 59, 90
education reforms 1, 5, 14, 23, 59, 61, 73, 86, 87, 117
education system 1–3, 5, 21–23, 27, 42, 45, 60, 63, 64, 66, 70–72, 74, 75, 86, 87, 90
educational assessment 2, 5, 16, 17, 22, 30, 44, 76, 79, 83, 88, 98, 117, 121
educational credentials 29, 46–48, 51
educational policy 16, 42, 44, 61, 91
educational researchers 17, 23, 70, 86, 121
educational transferability 29, 51
educators 3, 7, 11, 17, 23, 36, 41, 42, 44, 52–54, 60, 63, 70, 72, 86, 88, 91, 118, 121
end-of-term examination 8
English language learners, English as a second language or English as a foreign language 61, 98
E-portfolios 87
equitable learning opportunities 1, 59, 60
ethnic Chinese and Indian students 9
evaluation 1, 3, 4, 20, 22, 27–31, 34–38, 40, 42, 44, 46, 50, 51, 53, 70, 75, 77, 80, 85, 86, 98, 101, 108, 116
evidence centered design 121
evidence-based practice 72, 119, 120

evidentiary arguments 121
examinations 7–11, 23, 32–46, 48–54, 63, 64, 72–74
experiential learning 31, 121
experiential mood 104
experimentation 105, 106, 108, 111
extended communication 71

fables 29–31, 53, 122
facilitator of learning 117
Fazio, X. 22
feedback 11, 20, 31, 59, 62, 68, 81, 85, 116, 118–120
final paper 115, 116
Finnish model 74
First Nations, Métis, and Indigenous education 67, 99
formal assessment 27–29, 31, 50–52, 89
formal education 9, 27, 29, 37, 53
formative assessment 1, 12, 15, 17, 20, 21, 36, 59, 68, 70, 71, 75, 78, 81, 82, 85, 116, 118, 120, 121
formative classroom assessment data 16
framework for 21st century learning 66, 75
Fullan, M. 90
functions 2, 4, 9, 16, 32, 33, 39, 69, 75, 76, 78, 89

game-based assessments 20, 78, 121
Gamoran, A. 106
gatekeepers 29, 37, 38
GCE 'A' Level exam 9, 41, 63
GCE 'O' Level exam 23, 41, 44, 63, 72
genuine school (schole) 104
geopolitical 3, 4, 60, 121
Gipps, C. 9
global education reforms 1, 5, 23, 61, 86, 87, 117
Goh Chok Tong 71
grading 11, 27, 76, 104, 109
Greece 4
grit and resilience 12, 22, 74
growth mindset 10, 15, 59, 91, 119
guiding questions 116, 120
Gunn, S. 2
Guo, Shibao 34, 42, 51,
Guo, Yan 36, 42,
Guo, Yansheng 34
Guskey, T. 90
Guyana 39

Hargreaves, A. 59, 90
Harlen, W. 17, 18
high-achieving/high-performing education systems 5, 23, 74
higher education institutions 8, 11, 12, 61, 62, 66, 75–86, 120
higher-order competencies 2, 117
high-quality assessment 1, 7, 18, 22, 75, 78, 86–88, 90, 116, 120, 121
high-stakes national examinations 7, 9, 10, 63, 64
history/historical 2, 3, 4, 7, 31, 40, 41, 54, 97, 100
Hodge, K. A. 66
human rights 51, 52

immigrant professionals 28, 29, 46, 48, 50, 51
immigrant women 29, 48–50
immigrants' experiences (Canada) 46
immigration Canada 36, 51, 54, 61
inclusive learning environments 69, 99
independent and lifelong learners 74
Information, Communication, and Technology (ICT) 12, 22
initial teacher preparation 1–4, 7, 15, 22, 59–61, 75
inquiry-based pedagogies or inquiry-based learning 59, 60, 74
inservice teacher professional development programs 2, 3, 7, 15, 59, 91
inservice teachers 1–3, 7, 13, 15, 21–23, 59–61, 74–76, 84, 86, 87, 89–91, 117, 120
inspiring education 67, 71
instructional practice 1, 14–17, 20, 21, 59, 68, 75
instructors 10, 11, 13, 14, 32, 33, 37, 78, 88, 97, 98, 101, 104, 105, 108, 110, 115–119, 122
international assessments 5, 23, 60, 63–66, 86
investment 59, 60, 70–75
I.R.E./F. 20
issue-based design 98
item formats 10, 12

Jamaica 39, 41, 42, 44, 45
job interview 120
journal writing 107, 108

K–12 classrooms 15, 70
K–12 school curricula 1, 61
K–12 students 2, 16, 19, 22, 88, 89, 118

K–12 teachers 1, 17, 59
Klenowski, V. 2, 19
Klinger, D. 35
Knowledge, Skills, and Attributes (KSA) benchmarks 99, 100, 103, 108–110, 121
Koh, K. 3–5, 28, 36, 76–85, 88, 89, 119, 121

large-scale assessment 75, 81, 82
Lear, J. L. 66
learning and life skills 73
learning by doing 121
learning environment 8, 14, 21, 53, 69, 80, 81, 99
learning goals or outcomes 10, 15, 18, 19, 59, 67, 69, 71, 76–86, 90, 116, 117
learning process 14, 15, 18, 20, 21, 74, 75, 120
learning progression 121
learning sciences 121
Lee, Hsien Loong 72
liberal education 101
life chances of learners 29
Lingard, B. 13
linguistically and culturally diverse 2
lived experiences 28
London, N. 37–40, 42, 54
lower-order learning outcomes 10
Luke, A. 2, 13, 72

Malaysia 3, 7–9, 23, 28, 47, 62
Marks, H. M. 106
M.Ed. program 74, 76–84
managerial view of teachers 101
mathematics authentic assessment 89
measurement 12, 13, 16, 68, 76, 78–80, 84, 121
measurement errors 18,
Meighan, R. 37
metacognitive strategies 59, 107
Ministry of Education (MOE) 39, 42, 63, 67, 71–75, 87
motivation 18, 118

National Institute of Education (NIE) 13, 63, 72, 83
Newmann, F. 13, 69, 106,
Nicomachean ethics 103, 104
non-academic skills 10, 15, 67, 73

parents 7, 16, 17, 27, 28, 36, 39, 43, 50, 62, 63, 68, 70
partner teacher or mentor teacher 89

partnership for 21st century skills 66, 75
past learning experiences or previous educational experiences 14, 120
pedagogy 2, 7, 11, 13, 14, 20, 40, 59, 60, 62, 68, 70, 72–74, 86–89, 102, 117
peer assessment 18, 68
Pellegrino, J. W. 121
performance assessment 10, 20, 21, 59, 64, 76, 77, 81, 83
performance-based tasks 2, 65, 101
performance mindset 10, 118, 119
performance standards 1
personal transformation 103
philosopher 3, 45, 102, 104
philosophy of education 4, 11, 35, 97, 98, 101–111
Pieper, J. 102, 103
Pierre Hadot 102, 103
point system 46, 54
policies 3–5, 14, 23, 42, 46, 47, 51, 61, 72, 90, 91
policy borrowing 3
policymakers 3, 16, 19, 27, 30, 31, 60, 64, 68, 86, 116
Poonwassie, D. 37, 39, 40, 42
Popham, W. J. 15, 22
portfolio assessment 12, 87
post-colonial countries 3, 7
post-secondary institutions 27, 97, 100
post-secondary teaching 3, 45
practicum or field experience 44, 87, 89, 114, 115, 119
preservice teacher education program 3, 22
preservice teachers/student teachers/teacher candidates 1, 3, 4, 5, 14, 16, 17, 20, 22, 23, 33, 44, 88, 52, 60, 63, 76, 83, 87–89, 91, 98, 102, 108, 109, 111, 114–122
principles of sound assessment 2, 15, 78
problem-based learning 88, 97, 117
problem scenarios 5, 114, 116, 117, 120–122
problem solving 1, 10, 12, 14, 22, 60, 66, 67, 69, 81, 88, 117
professional career 101, 102, 105
professional development 2, 3, 5, 7, 15, 21–23, 49, 59–61, 63, 70–75, 77, 86–91, 117, 121
professional judgment 22, 62, 82
professional learning 21–23, 60, 63, 70, 74, 75, 86, 89–91, 120
professional teacher competences 98

INDEX

professional teaching standards   119
Program for International Student
    Assessment (PISA)   63–65, 86
programs of study   67, 71
Progress in International Reading Literacy
    Study (PIRLS)   63
project work   64, 71, 72
psychometric testing   11
psychometricians   121
purposes and functions   2, 4, 16, 75, 76, 78, 89
pursuit of wisdom   5, 6, 111

quality assessment for learning and
    teaching   116, 120

real-world contexts   22, 71, 117
realignment   69, 70
recommendations   5, 31, 61, 69, 74, 87–91, 114
reflections   7, 20, 120–122
reflective practitioners   78, 87
reflective thinking   88, 120
reliable   2, 18, 80
reproduction of facts and procedures   73
research-informed practice   118, 119
rich tasks   13
rote memorization   9, 60
rubric   11, 19, 76–78, 81, 82, 84, 110, 116, 118, 119, 121

Sahlberg, P.   86
Sawyer, R. K.   117
Schmidt, M.   59, 90
school administrators or leaders   13, 16, 17, 68, 70, 74–77
school-based assessment   72
school-based professional learning
    community   74, 86, 90
Science Practical Assessment (SPA)   64, 72
Science, Technology, Engineering, and
    Mathematics (STEM)   22, 65, 66, 98
self-assessment   59, 64, 108–110, 119, 120
self-directed learning   1, 10, 12, 22, 59, 60, 73, 88, 117
Shamugaratnam, Tharman   72, 73
Shepard, L.   17, 68–70
Shulman, L.   88, 117
Sierra Leone   37, 40
signature pedagogies   88, 117
Singapore   3–5, 7, 12, 13, 23, 60–67, 70–84

Singapore Examinations and Assessment
    Board (SEAB)   72
Singaporean schools   71, 72
Snyder, J.   88
social-constructivist learning   14, 68
sociocultural and political context   14, 23, 60, 121
socioemotional competencies   73
soft skills   69
spirit of inquiry   103
spiritual exercises   103, 107, 108
stakeholders   3, 4, 16, 18, 27, 28, 70, 86, 99, 116
standardized paper-and-pen tests   12, 15, 59
standards   1, 9–11, 15–19, 22, 23, 48, 61, 69, 75, 98, 115, 116–120
Stiggins, R.   2, 15–18
strategies   2, 3, 5, 7, 8, 14, 16, 20, 22, 23, 32, 36, 63, 64, 70, 889, 101, 108, 121
Strategies for Active and Independent
    Learning (SAIL)   64, 72
student achievement or performance   11, 15, 17–20, 38, 59, 60, 64, 65, 68, 70, 72,
Student Learning Assessments (SLAs)   62
student- or learner-centered pedagogical
    approaches   60, 88, 117
students' assignments   11, 120
students' learning   1, 11, 12, 15, 16, 18, 20, 21, 60, 62, 68, 71, 73–75, 78, 86, 89, 90
success criteria   68
Sumara, D.   90
Summa Theologica   104
summative assessments   10–12, 20, 21, 23, 31, 68, 73–75, 108, 118
survey-based approach   98

Tan, C.   73
task design   84, 106
Teach Less, Learn More (TLLM)   72, 73
teacher certification   1, 22, 75, 105, 110
teacher education   3, 5, 15, 22, 42, 44, 60, 62, 74, 75, 86, 87, 97–111, 121
teacher educators   3, 7, 17, 23, 70, 72, 86, 88, 91, 118, 121
teachers' capacity building   59, 77, 121
teaching   1–4, 10, 11, 13–16, 18, 20, 23, 30, 31, 33, 35, 36, 38, 44–46, 53, 54, 60, 62, 63, 68–70, 72, 74, 75, 79, 80, 83–88, 97–99, 101, 102, 104–107, 109–111, 114–120
teaching quality standards   75, 99

technology   16, 22, 31, 35, 42, 53, 65, 67, 80, 83, 98, 121
test developers   16, 121
tests   8–12, 15–17, 20, 30–32, 44, 45, 52, 59, 62, 68, 69, 73, 80, 121
Thinking Schools Learning Nation (TSLN)   63, 71, 72
transferability   4, 29, 46–48, 51
transformative intellectual activity   102
Trends in International Mathematics and Science Study (TIMSS)   63–65
Trinidad and Tobago   37, 39

UNESCO   29, 52
United Kingdom   17
United Nations   4, 29
United States/US   16, 22, 29, 34, 35, 37, 47, 48, 51, 65, 66, 86

universality   4, 29, 51

validity   19, 21, 47, 79, 121
value beyond school   106, 107
values   20, 27, 35, 37, 45, 66, 67, 73, 91, 108
Volante, L.   22
Vygotsky, L.   14

Wang, R.   53
ways of life   102–107, 109, 111
whole-class lectures   20
Wiggins, G.   69, 118
Wiliam, D.   17, 70
Willis, J.   2, 19–21
workbooks   8, 10
worksheets   8, 10
Wright, H.   37, 40, 42
Wyatt-Smith, C.   2

www.ingramcontent.com/pod-product-compliance
Lightning Source LLC
Chambersburg PA
CBHW061844300426
44115CB00013B/2504